COLLECTING FOSSILS

COLLECTING FOSSILS
Hold prehistory in the palm of your hand

Steve and Jane Parker

CONTRA COSTA COUNTY LIBRARY
Sterling Publishing Co., Inc.
New York

A QUARTO BOOK

Library of Congress Cataloging-in-Publication-Data is available
upon request.

Published by Sterling Publishing Co. Inc.
387 Park Avenue South
New York, NY 10016 - 8810

Distributed in Canada by Sterling Publishing c/o
Canadian Manda Group, One Atlantic Avenue, Suite 105 Toronto,
Ontario, Canada M6K 3E7

This book was designed and produced by
Quarto Publishing plc
6 Blundell Street
London N7 9BH

Project Editor Rebecca Moy
Editor John Farndon
Editorial Director Gilly Cameron Cooper

Art Editor Elizabeth Healey
Picture Researchers Miriam Hyman, Henny Letailleur
Designer Liz Brown
Assistant Art Director Penny Cobb
Photographer Chas Wilder
Illustrators Ann Tout, Wayne Ford
Art Director Moira Clinch

Manufactured in Hong Kong by
Regent Publishing Services Ltd
Printed in Hong Kong by
Winner Offset Printing Factory Ltd

ISBN 0-8069-9762-1

CONTENTS

Introducing Fossils

LITHOSTROTION

(above) was a colonial coral that grew in tangled masses on reefs in Mississippian and Pennsylvanian (Carboniferous) seas, 300 million years ago. The branches were formed from protective cases built by tiny animals called coral polyps (resembling sea anemones), one on top of another.

WHEN AN AGED RELATIVE reaches her 100th birthday, and recalls her childhood, a human lifetime may seem very long. Yet the Earth is 45 million times older! To demonstrate this, if you imagine the entire history of our planet were condensed into your own height, then:

• the Earth would form at your feet;
• the first microscopic signs of life would appear at the level of your knees;
• the first larger creatures, such as worms and jellyfish, would appear at the level of your neck;
• early fish would evolve at mouth height;
• dinosaurs, mammals, and birds would evolve over halfway up your forehead,
• and the whole of human history would be represented by a layer as thin as the hair lying flat on your head.

WHAT FOSSILS TELL US

How do we know all this? From fossils, the remains of plants, animals, and other living things, preserved in rocks and turned into stone.

The study of fossils shows how living things have changed, or evolved, over millions of years. From the first tiny and simple life-forms, they evolved into early plants, jellyfish, shellfish, fish, dinosaurs, flowers and trees, birds, and mammals. The fossil record is the story of life, written in the rocks.

Fossils also tell us much more than how living things have evolved—they show that the Earth's continents (main landmasses) have slowly moved around the surface of the planet over millions of years, coming together and then drifting apart, again and again. They also show how weather and climate have changed through the ages, from dry and desertlike, to hot, wet and steamy, to the intense cold of ice ages. And fossils show our own origins. They reveal that certain types of ape-like mammals gradually evolved into ourselves—humans.

TELLING THE TIME

To make sense of fossils, we need to tell the time. The Earth's immense prehistory is divided into a geologic timescale, shown on pages 8–9. This was worked out by pioneer geologists mainly during the 1800s. They recognized lengths of time called periods, from the characteristic types of rocks and fossils formed during them.

FOSSILS OF BIRDS *are extremely rare. Their thin and fragile bones were normally crushed, weathered and destroyed soon after death. An almost complete skeleton like this is even more exceptional, with the bones still in their relative positions, and linked together or articulated. This long-legged, plover-like wader Messelornis lived about 50 million years ago.*

Some periods are named after their types of rocks. For example, the Cretaceous Period is named for the thick layers of chalk laid down during its millions of years.

Other periods take their names from the place where the rocks were first studied. The sandstones and shales of the Devonian Period were closely examined in Devon in Southwest England. The rocks of the Jura Mountains between France and Switzerland gave their name to the Jurassic Period.

THE SCIENCE OF FOSSILS

Geology is the general name for the study of the Earth and its origins, structure, and rocks. Scientists who specialize in fossils are called paleontologists. They carefully search and dig for fossils around the world, clean and study them, and suggest what the animals and plants looked like when they were alive. They organize fossil collections in museums, and make models and recreations of dinosaurs and other prehistoric living things.

Anyone can get interested in fossils, start a collection, and become an expert. Indeed, there are millions of amateur fossilhunters around the world. They find fossils fascinating, informing, rewarding, and fun. Their work adds to the knowledge of the professionals, and helps to uncover the mysteries of long-extinct animals and plants. Now and again, an exceptional fossil makes international news. Its discoverer finds world fame—and perhaps fortune!

LEAF FOSSILS *(below) form when sediments such as silt covered the original leaves rapidly, before rotting or being eaten. Leaves of maidenhair trees show they have been almost unchanged for millions of years. The Gondwana tree Glossopteris provides evidence that several continents were once joined into one supercontinent—see page 41.*

Time, Life, and Fossils

WE ARE USED TO time being measured in minutes, hours, and days. But when we talk about fossils and the age of the Earth, these measurements are far too small. Geologic time is divided into four huge chunks called eras. These are split into periods—the fossil expert's "working units"—and cover 50-150 million years. Their beginning and end are marked by distinct changes in the rocks and the fossils they contain. The two most recent periods are subdivided into epochs.

PRECAMBRIAN
"Before the Cambrian"
Hadean Eon
4,550 to 3,800 mya
No signs of life (no fossils).
Archean Eon
3,800 to 2,500 mya
Small, simple life-forms such as bacteria, blue-green algae (cyanobacteria) in the sea (simplest life-forms, monerans).
Proterozoic Eon
2,500 to 540 mya
Soft-bodied animals such as worms, jellyfish, some sponges, large algae (seaweed).

PALEOZOIC ERA
"Ancient life"
Cambrian Period
540 to 505 mya
Rapid evolution of shelled sea animals, such as mollusks.
Trilobites and other hard-cased, joint-legged animals appear.
Ordovician Period
505 to 433 mya
Algae such as seaweeds become larger.
Shelled marine animals of many kinds.
First main vertebrates— jawless fish.

EARTH FORMED
approx 4,600 mya
4600

PRECAMBRIAN

PALEOZOIC ERA 540
Cambrian
505
Ordovician

433
Silurian

360 *Devonian*
Mississippian &
286 *Pennsylvanian*

245
MESOZOIC ERA

Permian *Triassic*

24

5

Silurian Period
433 to 410 mya
Many shelled animals— trilobites, nautiloids and other mollusks in the sea. Fish diversifying.
Devonian Period
410 to 360 mya
Fish and mollusks dominate the seas.
First land plants, followed by land animals such as millipedes, scorpions, insects, and amphibians.

Mississippian and Pennsylvanian Periods *(Carboniferous)*
360 to 286 mya
Huge forests of tree-ferns, giant insects, land amphibians.
First conifer trees.
First reptiles.

Permian Period
286 to 245 mya
Ends with mass extinction of many marine shelled animals, trilobites, mammal-like reptiles, and many other animals and plants.

MESOZOIC ERA
"Middle life"
Triassic Period
245 to 202 mya
Conifer trees more widespread.
Variety of reptiles dominate the land.
First dinosaurs and mammals.

Jurassic Period
202 to 144 mya
Conifers are the main large land plants.
Dinosaurs reach greatest size.
Ichthyosaurs and other reptiles take over the seas.
Pterosaurs dominate the skies.
First birds.

Cretaceous Period
144 to 65 mya
Dinosaurs continue to evolve.
Flowering plants (flowers, herbs, trees) evolve in middle of period, with similar spread of insects.
Ends with mass extinction of dinosaurs, pterosaurs, marine reptiles, ammonoids, many other mainly sea-dwelling shelled animals and plants.

CENOZOIC ERA
"Recent life"
Tertiary Period
65 to 2 mya

Paleocene Epoch
65 to 58 mya
Rapid evolution and spread of mammals and birds.
Eocene Epoch
58 to 37 mya
Whales, bats, first carnivores, other diverse mammals appear.
Oligocene Epoch
37 to 24 mya
Birds spread rapidly.
Many marine shelled animals die in "mini mass extinction".
Miocene Epoch
24 to 5 mya
Grasses and grazing mammals evolve, monkeys, bats, and sea mammals diversify.
Pliocene Epoch
5 to 2 mya
Giant mammals and giant land birds.
Evolution of humans.
Quaternary Period
2 mya to present day
Pleistocene Epoch
2 to 0.001 mya (10,000 years ago)
True fossils shade into sub-fossils (which are not fully mineralized).
Giant mammals of Ice Ages.
Early humans.
Holocene Epoch
0.001 mya (10,000 years ago) to present day
End of main Ice Ages and rise of human civilizations. Prehistory becomes history.

202
Jurassic

144
Cretaceous

65

58

37

← **Tertiary Period**

CENOZOIC ERA

2

10,000 YEARS AGO

Quaternary Period ➡

A Brief History of Fossils

Fossils are the remains of once-living things which have been preserved for many thousands, millions, or even hundreds of millions of years. Museums may seem full of them, in rows of glass cases and boxes, but in fact, fossils are very rare. Countless numbers of plants, animals, and other organisms (living things) once thrived and later died on Earth, over the past 3,500 million years. Only a very tiny fraction of them were preserved in some way as fossils.

This is because nature recycles things almost perfectly. Practically every part of each living thing, dead or alive, eventually becomes food or nutrients for another living thing. Many plants and animals are eaten whole by their predators, with leftover parts being consumed by scavengers. Any rotting remains are broken down by fungi and bacteria, and go back into the soil. Even very tough parts like bones and shells eventually crumble, becoming nutrients for new plant growth—there is rarely any waste.

A CHANCE EVENT

Fossils are only made if the processes of eating, rotting, and recycling are interrupted; they rarely are. It usually happens when the remains of an organism are quickly covered in some way, keeping out scavengers, in conditions where there is little decay, so the remains rot away very slowly.

This can happen because of chance events such as a flash flood that washes silt onto a riverbank, a desert storm that blankets the landscape with sand, or a sliding avalanche of mud on the seabed. The covering layer of tiny particles of silt, sand, or mud, called sediments, stops the circulation of water and oxygen. This prevents decay. Then gradually, over a long time, the organism's remains change into fossils (*see pp. 12–13*).

Only the hardest parts of organisms—bones, teeth, claws, horns, scales, shells, seeds, and wood—stay intact long enough for this to happen. Skin, guts, petals, and other soft parts are soon crushed beyond recognition.

Fossils *(above) have always intrigued people— this carved wooden clerical shield is adorned with three ammonites. It was not until the seventeenth century, however, that people began to suspect the true origins of these pleasing patterned objects.*

HIPPOPOTAMUS JAW AND TUSK

(right) is a relatively young fossil. It is less than two million years old, from the Pleistocene Epoch of the Quaternary Period. The long root of the tusk, or canine tooth, is revealed by the worn jawbone, which also contains two molar or cheek teeth for chewing.

OTHER METHODS OF PRESERVATION

• **As mummies** Remains are preserved in very dry conditions, such as in desert caves, which prevent rotting.

• **In amber** Some trees, mainly conifers, ooze a thick, sticky liquid called sap or resin, which sets as a hard lump called amber. Tiny creatures, such as flies and spiders, and windblown pollen and seeds, get caught in it (*see p. 43*).

• **In tar** In some places, thick and sticky tar oozes naturally from the ground, forming pools and lakes. Animals can be trapped in this tar, which preserves them.

• **In ice** We use freezing temperatures to preserve our meat and other food. This happened in nature too, when animals and plants were frozen into ice during the Ice Ages.

FOSSILS IN STORAGE *(right) bear labels describing their identities, the sites where they were found, their age, and other important information. These are organized by type, with similar animals in the same drawer—in this example, molluscs and similar shellfish. Another option is to group a selection of organisms, including plants and animals, from the same time*

How Fossils Form

IT IS EXCITING to find the fossils of a big animal like a dinosaur or a saber-tooth cat, but most fossils are of shelled sea creatures. There are four main reasons for this:

Firstly, throughout prehistory, most of the Earth was covered by seas and oceans—as it is today. So there were far fewer land animals and plants than there were ocean animals.

Secondly, for millions of years of prehistory, the commonest animals in the sea were shelled creatures. Marine animals such as whales and seals evolved much more recently and they have been naturally fewer in number.

Thirdly, only hard parts usually form fossils, and the shells of most shellfish are very hard indeed.

Fourthly, conditions at the bottom of the sea are most likely to form fossils, compared to conditions on land, where scavenging and weathering destroy many remains.

THE RAREST FOSSILS
(above) include those of soft-bodied creatures like jellyfish. Their floppy bodies disintegrate within hours unless a chance event such as a mud slide occurs.

TINY AND SIMPLE ORGANISMS *(below) such as sponge-like stromatoporids, sponges, calcareous algae, and of course corals, built huge reefs in ancient seas, as they do today. The rocks preserve their minute details.*

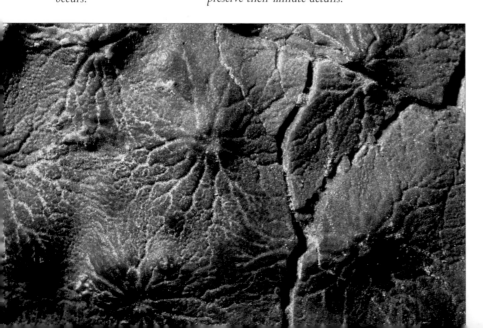

1   A shelled sea creature such as an ammonite lived in the sea, hunting and escaping from danger and looking for breeding partners.

6   The ammonite shell underwent the same process. It also changed into rock. This happened very slowly, as every tiny piece and particle of it was chemically altered into rock minerals, by the process of permineralization. It took millions of years, but the shell kept its overall shape.

2   The creature died. Its flesh and soft parts were quickly eaten by scavengers such as crabs and fish, who picked the shell clean.

3   The hard shell lay on the seabed. It was slowly covered by tiny particles of mud and silt, settling from the water, which prevented further decaying.

4   More and more sediments settled, forming thicker layers, and burying the hard shell ever deeper. This continued for thousands of years.

5   Gradually the pressing weight of the layers above, and chemical changes of the particles themselves, started to cement the sediments together, to form solid rock. This is called petrifaction.

7   There were huge earth movements and earthquakes, as one continent collided with another. The rocks of the seabed were crumpled and pushed upwards.

8   The rocks were lifted so high that they came above sea level, to form hills on dry land.

9   The rocks were now exposed to the forces of weather and nature. These gradually wore away or eroded the overlying layers.

10   Finally erosion uncovers or "weathers out" part of the fossil. A passing fossil collector notices it sticking up out of the ground…and a fossil is discovered!

What Fossils Tell Us

FOSSILS TELL US A great deal about extinct animals and plants. However, many fossils are only parts or fragments of the original whole body and often their shapes have been distorted by rock pressures and movements— so you may have to carry out detective work on unfamiliar specimens.

THE ORGANISM ITSELF

Fossils show the size and shape of hard parts, like an animal's bones or a tree's woody trunk and branches. Paleontologists compare these with equivalent parts in similar species alive today, so that the original organism can be identified.

MARKS MEAN MUCH

Many fossils show small features such as lumps and scars, which help to fill in details of the soft body parts. Marks on a fossil bone or shell reveal where the animal's muscles and ligaments were once anchored. Holes in a bone show where nerves and blood vessels passed through. The way that bones or parts of a shell fit together, and the shapes of the joints between them can suggest how the animal moved when alive. Both tree trunks and fish scales form growth rings as time passes and their owner gets older. These are sometimes preserved in fossils, showing the specimen's age at death.

ANIMAL DROPPINGS
(below) fossilize by turning to stone. They can be cracked or split to reveal their contents, such as undigested bits of animal bones and teeth, or tough plant parts like conifer needles and cones, showing the animal's last meal.

TEETH AND FOOD

The size and shape of fossil teeth, when compared with those of living animals, indicate the food that a prehistoric creature would have eaten. Tiny scratches and wear marks on the fossil teeth suggest certain foods, such as tough roots. Again, these are identified by comparison with micro-marks on the teeth of living animals. Tooth marks on a fossil bone or shell indicate which predator ended the victim's life.

Rarely, hard parts of an animal's last meal, such as bones, fish scales, or plant seeds, become fossils as the guts around them rot away.

CONTINENTAL DRIFT

Fossils of the seed fern plant called *Glossopteris* and of animals such as the reptile *Lystrosaurus*, are found in places that are widely separated today—like the two continents of South America and Africa. The probable answer is that long ago, when these plants and animals lived, the land masses were joined together. Piecing together this evidence, from hundreds of plant and animal fossils, shows how the continents have drifted around the globe, come together, and separated again over millions of years.

GLOSSOPTERIS *(above) provides strong evidence of continental drift. From evidence in the world today, different continents have their own types of plants and animals. But* **Glossopteris** *fossils are found on landmasses which are now far apart, suggesting they were once joined.*

TRACE FOSSILS

Some fossils derive, not from the plants or animals themselves, but from other evidence left behind by them. These are called trace fossils and include:
• Coprolites, or fossilized droppings. These have long since turned to stone, so they are not soft and smelly! They indicate the types of food eaten, and the size and shape of the animal's guts.
• Burrows, holes, and tunnels. Many ancient rocks from seashores show where worms and shellfish have bored into them.
• Footprints, paw marks, claw scrapes, and tail drags left in soft soil, sand, or mud.
• Nests, eggs, egg cases, and similar objects.

A DINOSAUR EGG *(below) has a particular shape and size according to the type of dinosaur that laid it. The connection between a dinosaur species and its egg usually relies on proximity—finding fossils of adults and eggs together or near each other.*

How and Where to Find Fossils

FOSSILS ARE LIKE WINDOWS on the past, or snapshots of prehistory. Every fossil fragment has a story to tell, involving exciting detective work. Fossil finding, identifying, and collecting are themselves big business. There are fossil auctions, fossil shops, and people who make a living from fossil-hunting. For example, engineers need a knowledge of fossils and geology when planning to dig foundations for a skyscraper, or drill for oil.

BE SPECIALIZED

Fossils are incredibly varied and widespread—no single person can know about them all, but one way to start is to choose your own area of interest. It may be the fossils in the rocks of your locality, fossils of a particular group of animals or plants, or fossils from a certain period of time.

BE PRACTICAL

Dinosaur fossil bones may look exciting in a museum, but they weigh tons, take years to dig out and clean up, and occupy a lot of space—so stay practical! Remember that smaller fossils are easier to extract, carry home, and display. Specimens such as the tiny tooth of an early mammal or the small scale of an unusual fish can be more valuable than the bigger fossils.

BE GEOLOGIC

Visit your local museum, nature center or geology club. Find out about the landscape, study the specimens and samples of stones and boulders, and learn about the various types of rocks. There are three main kinds:
• Igneous rocks form when molten rock, such as lava from a volcano, cools and goes solid. They almost never contain fossils.
• Metamorphic rocks form when great heat and pressure change other rocks. They rarely contain fossils, since these are destroyed by the changes.
• Sedimentary rocks form when tiny particles of sediments, such as sand,

ERODING CLIFFS

(below), with rocks laid down in layers or strata, are ideal places to hunt for fossils. But they are also dangerous, with loose boulders and life-threatening rockfalls. Always take full safety precautions.

THE WORLD-FAMOUS MORRISON FORMATION
*Utah, U.S. (left) has provided spectacular fossil finds, including complete skeletons of giant dinosaurs like **Allosaurus**, **Apatosaurus,** and **Stegosaurus** from the Jurassic Period.*

silt, mud, and clay, are pressed and cemented together (*see pp. 12–13*). These are the kinds which may contain fossils—especially limestones, sandstones, shales, slates, claystones, marls, loesses, flints, and coals.

BE BIOLOGIC

There are many groups of plants and animals, but only some leave plentiful fossils. If you are familiar with their relatives alive today, you are more likely to recognize their fossils from the past. So look at books, visit botanical gardens and zoos, and go on nature walks. This helps to provide background knowledge, and to make your fossil-hunting more successful.

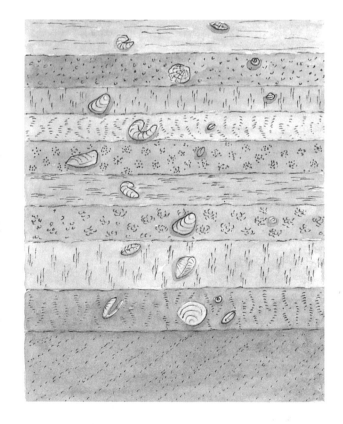

DATING FOSSILS BY FOSSILS *(right). Some plants and animals, especially certain molluscs, were very common during long periods of prehistory—their fossils abound, and are well-known. They show an evolutionary series, or sequence of progressive yet distinctive changes through time. The presence of these common fossils in rocks allows dating of a rock—and of any other fossils in it. These fossils are called marker, guide, or indicator fossils.*

Plan Your Fossil-Hunting Trip

Plan your fossil-hunting trips in advance. Otherwise you may end up looking for the wrong things in the wrong places. Careful planning helps to ensure safety. Check that you will be visiting a suitable site at a safe time. Always tell someone where you are going, and when you plan to return. Then, if something goes wrong, that person will be able to organize help. Forward planning will ensure you take the right equipment to extract your finds quickly and easily, enabling you to be home by early evening.

THE IMPORTANCE OF MAPS

Begin by studying maps of your area. Look at the usual countryside maps, and also at the geologic maps kept in libraries, museums, nature centers, or survey organizations.

Geologic maps show the types and ages of rocks exposed at the surface of the ground, using color-coded shading. A book such as a geology field guide is also useful to identify the various types of rocks and stones.

Focus on sedimentary rocks such as limestones and sandstones, which may contain fossils. You can see actual specimens in the displays at your nearby museum, nature center, or rock-and-fossil store.

LIMESTONE

EXPERT HELP

Almost every region has a neighborhood fossil or geology group. You can gain valuable knowledge by talking to the experts, and listening to their experiences and advice. They often organize trips to particular sites where fossils are plentiful. These supervised visits are useful practise for fossil-hunting, familiarizing you with features and signs to look for.

Most clubs know how to get permission to visit sites. They may even organize digs in restricted places such as privately owned quarries or mines. They can suggest gaps in the body of knowledge for a region, which your collection could fill, making a long-lasting contribution to paleontology.

CLIFF OUTCROPS
(left), as in these sandstone formations, often provide rich pickings for fossil hunters. Some sandstones formed in deserts, where conditions preserved the bodies of plants and animals. Other sandstones were once sand on prehistoric beaches and shallow seabeds.

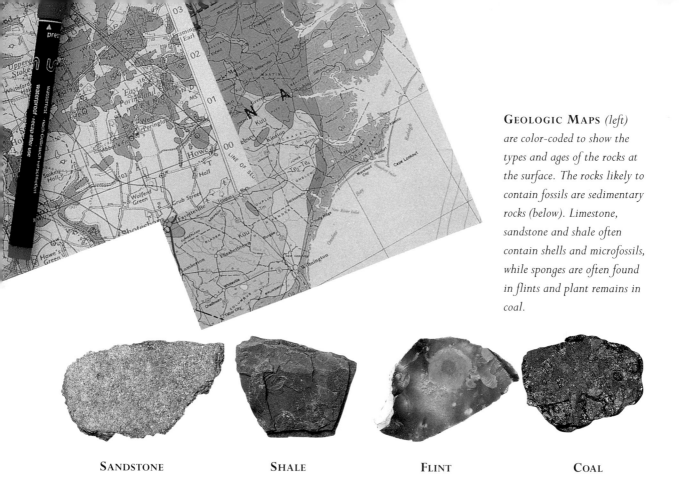

Geologic Maps *(left)*
*are color-coded to show the
types and ages of the rocks at
the surface. The rocks likely to
contain fossils are sedimentary
rocks (below). Limestone,
sandstone and shale often
contain shells and microfossils,
while sponges are often found
in flints and plant remains in
coal.*

SANDSTONE　　　**SHALE**　　　**FLINT**　　　**COAL**

KEEP YOUR EYES OPEN!

Even when you are not on a proper
fossil-hunting trip—keep your eyes open!
Develop an instinct for recognizing fossils, and
places where they might be.
• Look up—many buildings are constructed
from blocks of sedimentary rock, such as
sandstone. Fossils may be embedded in their
surfaces.
• Look down—old paving stones, slates, and
stone steps may show signs of fossils.
• Look around—stone walls, rock posts, and
even lumps of coal can reveal beautiful fossils.
• Look near and far—wherever you go, try to
visit fossil collections.

UNDER YOUR FEET *(above) might be paving slabs
or flooring tiles made from fossil-rich stone. They
produce attractive patching, swirling, and other effects.
The way the slabs are sliced and polished reveals some
fossils' internal details.*

Look in the Right Places!

THERE IS NO INSTANT WAY to identify a fossil-bearing rock—other than to spot a fossil in it. However, there are various guidelines you can follow.

THE TYPE OF ROCK

Fossils are nearly always found in sedimentary rocks (*see p. 17*), particularly those formed under water. So look for the characteristic layers, beds, or strata that make up sedimentary rocks. Over millions of years, intense pressures and earth movements may bend or twist the layers or strata. Slight distortion does not matter too much, but avoid intensely squeezed or folded layers.

FOSSILS ABOUND

along some rocky shores (right). The eroding effects of tides, crashing waves, hot sun, windblown particles, heavy rain, and rolling boulders continually flakes and cracks the stone to expose new specimens, like the coffee-table-sized ammonoid in the foreground.

DATING FOSSILS

Usually, a fossil is as old as the rock around it. Finding the age of rocks and their fossils is called dating. It is vital for fitting fossils into the framework of geologic time. Dating is done in two main ways—as described here.

• Absolute dating

Sensitive scientific equipment can measure certain features of a rock, such as the tiny amounts of natural radioactivity (such as radiocarbon) or magnetism in it, or the levels of certain minerals, such as fluorine. This gives an age in thousands or millions of years, with certain limits.

• Relative dating

Sedimentary rocks are usually formed in layers or strata, the oldest at the bottom and most recent on top. This gives their ages relative to each other. Also, certain types of rocks form in characteristic orders or sequences. So identifying several successive layers can show their place in the overall timescale.

THE AGE OF ROCK

Geologic maps show the general age of rocks exposed at the surface, usually by periods of the geologic timescale (*see pp. 8–9*). For most fossil hunters, rocks of the Cambrian Period and later are most productive.

Certain periods in prehistory left more and better fossils than others. The Mississippian and Pennsylvanian Periods (Carboniferous) are famed for their plentiful fossils of ferns and other plants, huge insects, and amphibians.

THE EXPOSURE OF ROCK

Search for fossils where suitable rocks are bare and exposed, and where the rock is being worn away rapidly by the forces of weathering or erosion. This helps to expose fresh parts of the rock in a continuing process. Places where this happens naturally include rocky outcrops, rocky hills and mountains, stone-strewn seashores, cliffs, canyons and valleys, and the rocky shores of lakes and rivers. Human activity has created other suitable sites—stone quarries, mines, cuttings, and excavations. But make safety a priority in places like these (*see pp. 22–25*).

QUARRIES *(below) are ideal places to look for fossils. You may choose a quarry conveniently close to home, or one where rocks of a certain age are exposed. But always get permission and take precautions.*

Getting Equipped

THE FIRST STEP is to contact the landowner of the site you wish to visit. Explain exactly what you wish to do, and why. The local fossil, geology, or archeology organization can help with this.

You may have to apply for certain permissions or licenses. You may also be asked to sign forms agreeing to abide by certain conditions. Get the advice of a qualified person if you are asked to do this.

At a working site, such as a quarry, follow the instructions of the manager. He or she will know the best times to visit, usually when machines and staff are not active. Again, you may have to sign legal disclaimer forms, and wear protective clothing such as a hard hat.

VISITING SITES

(below) where rocks are exposed by erosion, either natural or man-made, is an absorbing pastime. Safety precautions can prevent accidents as you concentrate on the rocks and their fossils.

PRECAUTIONS

• Do not visit sites alone—you should go in a group of three to four people, with at least one adult.

• Tell someone back at base exactly where you are going and when you expect to return.

• Take identification, licenses, permissions, and money as required. A mobile phone is extremely helpful for emergencies.

• In a remote place, take suitable equipment and supplies (*see pp. 24–25*).

STAYING SAFE

Cracked and eroding rocks can be unstable and dangerous. Never climb a loose or crumbling cliff, a quarry face, a hillside of jumbled stones and boulders, or a steep gravel bank. Surfaces like these can slide or collapse, and cause injury or death. Instead, search along the base. There should be plenty of rocks to keep you busy. Listen for any cracks or rumbles that suggest a landslide or cliff-fall. Near these places, wear a hard hat, just in case.

THE IMPORTANCE OF CONSERVATION

Any trip to a natural place involves caring
for the wildlife and environment.

• Avoid unnecessary damage to the area and
its surroundings.

• Repair and replace as best you can.

• Do not disturb wild plants or animals, or
farm crops and livestock.

• Avoid starting fires.

• Leave farm gates as you found them, open
or closed.

• Do not leave litter or mess.

• Avoid digging as much as possible.

• Never take more than you need.

STEEP OR SLIPPERY

You should also avoid searching on slippery
surfaces, especially wet or mossy rocks, and near
steep slopes or cliff edges. Steer clear, too, of
sites such as cliff faces and those containing
potholes. Soft mud and quicksand are hazards to
avoid at all times, especially in swampy or coast
areas.

   Near the sea, you should always make sure
you will not be cut off by the incoming tide—if
you're venturing along the coast, check that
there is a clear path back. Beware, too, of
exposure to extreme weather conditions—and
sunburn (*see pp. 24–25*).

COASTAL CLIFFS (*right*) *may literally be made of fossils.
But conditions here are extremely hazardous—a sheer face,
damp and slippery surfaces, loose stones, possible gusts of
high wind—and the potential to be trapped by the tide or
hit by falling rocks. Stay away!*

Heading for the Field

FOSSIL-HUNTING CAN BE HARD, heavy work, so the right equipment will help greatly—tools are described in more detail on pages 26–27. Field equipment, which you carry on the trip, is usually minimal and lightweight.

TRANSPORTATION

A successful day's digging may produce a considerable weight of fossils. So make suitable transportation arrangements. If you are on foot, take the safest path, which may not be the shortest. Do not struggle to carry one heavy load, since you may fall or suffer injury; if possible, split the load and carry it in several journeys, or come back later with others to help.

CLOTHES AND CONDITIONS

Make sure your clothing suits the weather conditions. Several thinner garments can be removed or replaced, layer by layer, as the temperature changes. Always carry a waterproof, hooded outer garment, like an anorak, in case of rain or high wind, or if you get stranded. This helps to prevent exposure and hypothermia.

Fierce sun can be equally harmful, causing hyperthermia. To prevent sunburn use sunscreen lotions, wear a hat that protects your head and the back of your neck, and light clothing to cover your skin. In addition, rig up a tent, sheet, or large umbrella over the main working area for shade, and sip plenty of fluids to avoid dehydration.

OMO VALLEY, ETHIOPIA *(below) yielded fossils of prehistoric humans and their tools, shedding light on our own origins. But it is a harsh, remote and forbidding region, where fossil-digging is hard, hot work. All supplies, including food and water, must be brought long distances across a scorched, rugged landscape.*

THE FIELD TRIP (right) *will be more successful if it's carefully organized. Attention to detail makes sure that items are not forgotten at a crucial stage.*

JOIN THE PROFESSIONALS!

Many well-known fossil sites have established digs where professional paleontologists organize and advise teams of volunteers. They are usually very pleased to have extra help. Joining them is an excellent way to learn first hand and gain experience from the experts.

Never disturb an organized dig, or let children or dogs do so. You could spoil the carefully selected piles of rocks, drawings and records, and months of painstaking work.

Wear heavy-duty boots or shoes to protect your feet and support them when you are in awkward positions. Hard hats, knee pads, tough gloves, and plastic goggles offer extra protection.

OTHER USEFUL EQUIPMENT

• **Tape measure and compass** To check a fossil's size and exact location.
• **Local maps** Both a hiker's map, and a geologic survey map.
• **Camera** To record the site and scene (do not forget the film!).
• **Field notebook and pencil** For records, sketches of the specimen and site, and other vital information.
•**Backpack** To carry equipment and specimens while leaving your hands free.

Always wear a hard hat around cliff faces, quarries and any loose rocks.

Thickened gloves prevent fingers being hammered or squashed by boulders.

A weatherproof coat is essential in unpredictable climates.

Never chip rock without some form of eye protection such as plastic goggles.

Notepad and pencil are vital to record place, time, finds and future potential of a site.

A strong pair of boots protect against bad weather and falling or rolling rocks.

The Right Tools for the Job

ABONE, CLAW, OR SHELL from a recently dead animal is quite lightweight. But fossils of these objects are solid rock, and much heavier. They are often embedded in hard surrounding rock. The right tools, kept in good condition, make the job of extracting fossils easier.

The following list describes tools needed for a thorough, long-term dig. As you gain experience, you may find that you can make do with fewer tools which are easier to carry, especially on smaller digs.

For a first visit to the site, you may need only a hammer and trowel, a couple of specimen bags, and your notebook. You can get some idea of the types of rocks and likely fossils, and work out what you need for later visits. If the rocks are very hard, you may need larger hammers and chisels. Smaller, more delicate tools suit softer rocks and fossils that split more easily.

Share the carrying with others, and do not rush. You may come upon a great find and want to extract it at once, but it's probably been there for thousands of years!

• **CHISEL AND MALLET**
Chisels come in a range of sizes to cope with large-scale or fine, detailed work. They apply concentrated pressure to a rock to make it crack. A heavy rubber-headed mallet gives a cushioned blow, with a minimum of shock, and can also be used for tapping the chisels and dislodging soft rocks.

• **TROWEL** *For softer rocks, widening cracks and removing soil, sand, mud, or similar debris.*

• **GEOLOGIST'S HAMMER** *The key tool, pictured below, has one flat surface and a sharper pick-end for chisel-like blows. Choose one that is not too heavy, so you can easily manage it.*

FOSSIL COLLECTING
(left) calls for ingenuity and improvization. This adapted backpack makes a comfortable way of transporting finds. The specimens can be wrapped in padding and wedged into the large containers, secured with elastic straps, so they are not rubbed or knocked together.

• **SIEVES** *Separate small fossils such as teeth or shells from even smaller particles of soil, sand, silt, and mud.*

• **SMALL SPADE** *For bulk removal of soil or debris. A small pick may be useful where the rock is hard.*

• **PAINTBRUSH** *For removing dust and sand from delicate specimens.*

• **WIRE BRUSH** *For rough cleaning of unimportant, resistant material.*

• **HAND LENS** *For a close view of small fossils and the details on larger ones.*

• **CONTAINERS** *A variety of lightweight bags and boxes, with newspaper or paper towel for packing stop specimens from rolling about. Sticky labels and a pencil identify their contents.*

• **PLASTER JACKET** *Plaster of Paris and sacking, or specially made plaster bandages (as used by medical staff), support and protect specimens during removal and transportation.*

EXTRACTING A FOSSIL

1 *Brush around the specimen to clear the surface so you can identify it. If it does not fall out of the surrounding rock, or matrix, try to estimate how much of the fossil is embedded.*

2 *Gently chisel away the rock around the specimen, leaving plenty of spare matrix. Split off chunks with the hammer and chisel, using the rock's natural cracks, cleavage lines, and bedding planes. Examine the pieces as you go.*

3 *Work your way around the specimen, aiming to loosen it within a block of rock. You can do the fine work and cleaning later, in comfort.*

4 *If parts of the fossil are very soft, delicate, or crumbly, stabilize their surfaces with glue, resin, or specially made fixative (shellac, or similar).*

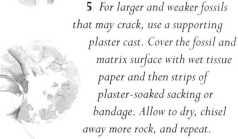

5 *For larger and weaker fossils that may crack, use a supporting plaster cast. Cover the fossil and matrix surface with wet tissue paper and then strips of plaster-soaked sacking or bandage. Allow to dry, chisel away more rock, and repeat.*

6 *At each stage, note details and measurements of the matrix and fossil. Sketch the area, take photographs, and record other important information.*

Starting Your Collection

Finding fossils "in the field" is only part of the fun of establishing a collection. Back "in the lab," your best specimens will need cleaning, identifying, cataloging, and storing or displaying. This is called curating.

A fully equipped paleontology laboratory would be ideal. But you can produce an excellent fossil display with much less space and equipment. Secondhand stores, yards sales, flea markets, and auctions are good places to find suitable old closets, chests, drawers, shelves, tables, chairs, and tools.

THE TRUE BEAUTY *of a fossil is revealed only after patient work, using ever finer tools to remove the surrounding rock matrix. Heavy-handedness can ruin a good specimen.*

THE WORKBASE

Prepare a work space for extracting and cleaning your fossils. A whole room may be a luxury, but a counter top in a kitchen or basement will do as well. A roomy closet or two are also important. Have areas for different tasks, such as large-scale extraction, fine cleaning, identification, and study.

The floor may get wet or chipped by falling bits of rock, so cover it with old rugs or newspaper if it is likely to suffer damage. A sink with running water, the larger the better, is an advantage, but you can use a large bowl.

An electricity supply is virtually a must for lighting the room, and it is important to have proper heating and perhaps power tools available.

SOME USEFUL EQUIPMENT

- *Safety goggles*
- *Gloves (such as gardening gloves)*
- *Paintbrushes of various sizes*
- *Tools for cleaning, such as picks and scrapers (see following pages)*
- *Chemicals for cleaning (see following pages)*
- *Large magnifier with stand, or a binocular microscope for close work*
- *Vise or sand tray to hold specimen*
- *Reference books such as fossil field guides and identification books*
- *Notebook and pencil*
- *Camera*
- *Paper towels or tissues*
- *Cotton balls*
- *Rags*
- *Newspaper*

WORKING CONDITIONS

People work best in a comfortable environment, warm but not hot, draft-free but well-ventilated, with plenty of natural light. Fossils should be kept in dry conditions. Arrange a suitable chair or stool at the correct height for your work surface, to prevent backache or a sore neck. Wall posters or pictures of natural areas, fossils, animals, and plants are both decorative and handy for reference.

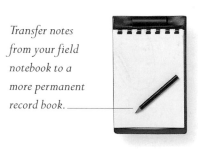

Transfer notes from your field notebook to a more permanent record book.

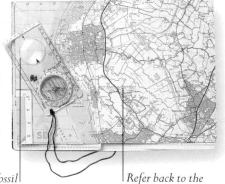

A compass gives the orientation of each fossil as it lay in the rock. This may help to explain the conditions under which the organisms died.

Refer back to the maps to check the exact position of each fossil find.

SURFACES AND STORAGE

Big fossils are heavy, and hammer blows produce great pressure. So work surfaces should be hard-topped, strong, and stable. To protect a high-quality surface, cover it with pieces of wood, newspapers, or old trays.

You need shelves, closets, and other storage space for tools, equipment, uncleaned fossils, and finished specimens. As your collection grows, you can put your best fossils on display, and store the rest in padded, labelled, and cataloged boxes or drawers. Keep large specimens on low, sturdy shelves.

Put your reference books, notepads, and smaller tools where they are handy. You can hang tools on adjustable pin boards or put them in trays. Make sure that sharp tools are safely away from children. Store dangerous chemicals and liquids in a safe closet, preferably metal and lockable.

Good lighting is essential over the workbench, especially as you progress to examine fine details.

Keep often-used equipment easily to hand, such as a hand lens, forceps, ruler, and probe.

A noticeboard is always useful for notes, reminders, charts, and photographs.

Store chemicals in small sealed containers in locked cupboards, to prevent misuse and accidents.

A dedicated workspace makes fossil preparation easier, because you can leave out half-prepared specimens. It's also important to keep work surfaces clear and tidy.

Keep record books, identification guides and specimens in drawers or cupboards, or on shelves.

The ever-present notepad and pencil is your basis for expanding jottings made in the field into permanent record books and a catalog system.

Protective equipment such as goggles and gloves are still necessary even when working in the workroom.

Will it be Worth the Work?

WHEN YOU RETURN FROM your field trip, back to your workbase, try to unpack your specimens before you forget what your quickly jotted labels and notes mean!

Close examination under a magnifying lens helps to identify the specimen and any special features.

A label should accompany any specimen, as it progresses from its original extraction to its final display.

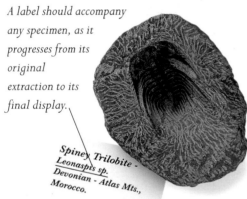

Spiney Trilobite -
Leonaspis sp.
Devonian - Atlas Mts.,
Morocco.

Spiney Trilobite -
Leonaspis sp.
Devonian - Atlas Mts.,
Mor...

This specimen is packed with its label, ready for long-term storage. It will be listed in the collection catalog.

1 ASSESSMENT

Look carefully at each fossil you bring home. After more detailed study, a fossil may not look quite as exciting as it did in the field. Or you may notice something special that you missed first time. Take into account any missing parts, breaks, or distortions, which could make it less worthwhile to clean in detail and display the fossil.

2 CATALOGING

Enter each specimen into your cataloging system. This may be an index card file box, or a computer, or both—one backing up the other. The sort of information needed includes:

• Catalog number, unique to every fresh specimen.
• Date and place where the fossil was collected.
• Type and age of the surrounding rocks.
• Provisional identification, which can be very broad at this stage, such as "mollusk" or "fern."
• Special features or important notes, such as the type of rock exposure and weathering, and the fossil's orientation.

You can put a sticky label summarizing this information on the specimen, or include it on a slip of paper. Keep the more extensive details in your card system or computer files.

3 TEMPORARY STORAGE

As each fossil is cataloged, place it in temporary storage, along with any drawings and photographs you made in the field. If the fossil has been set in plaster, do not remove it until you are ready to prepare it fully. You do not have to rush to prepare and display every specimen. Take each stage carefully and deliberately, or you may waste time on fossils that are not truly worth it.

4 EXAMINATION

The fossil may be free from bits of rock sticking to it, or it may need to be extracted (*see pp. 32–33*). When the whole specimen is exposed and cleaned, you can examine it in detail and probably identify it more fully. In addition to the identification guide later in this book, consult more detailed reference books.

5 IDENTIFICATION

For most amateur collections, identification does not have to be too detailed. Trying to reach a detailed level, such as a particular species or genus (group of species), is often tricky. Fossils are usually fragmentary and distorted, so identification may involve guesswork. It may help to take the specimen to a nearby museum.

THE FINISHED SPECIMEN *(below) has surrounding rock neatly shaped and decorated. There is no need to remove every fragment of matrix from a fossil leaving a lump adds interest and does not hide information, for example, if it is on the right side and the left side is exposed.*

...amily, species or type

Cleaned and prepared fossil specimen

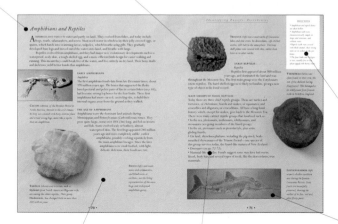

HOW TO USE THIS BOOK

The second half of this book covers all the main fossil groups, starting with plants and then moving through invertebrate animals and vertebrate animals.

Field notes: show you points to look out for when on a fossil-hunting trip.

Artist's impression of the plant or creature in life.

Text describes background to major fossil groups.

Fossil specimen in the rock it was found in.

The Fossil from the Rock

BEFORE TRYING TO EXTRACT a fossil that is embedded in its rock, or matrix, pause for thought. Which is the best technique? There are many different methods, physical and chemical.

The general rule is: Do as little as possible. Choose the least physical or "softest" method first. The more you handle and work on a specimen, the greater the chance there is of scratching, or breaking it. Try your proposed method on a "spare" specimen first.

PREPARATION

Work on a firm surface in well-lit surroundings. Support the fossil in a sand tray or wooden jig, or clamped into a vise with soft wood for protection. Think safety. Wear gloves and eye protectors. Brush the specimen clean, study it carefully, and consider your extraction plan.

Work slowly and patiently. Brush, chip, or scrape away from the fossil and yourself to avoid slips. As you get closer to the fossil's surface, use softer and finer tools, and work under a supported magnifying glass.

CLEANING A FOSSIL *(left) can take months or years, especially for a large and / or important specimen destined for professional scrutiny and public display. This technician is picking out matrix, speck by speck, with a fine probe or needle, from within the fossilized upper jaw of the dinosaur* **Allosaurus**. *This was a huge and fierce tyrannosaur-like meat-eater from the late Jurassic Period.*

RELIEFING *(left) involves carefully chipping, abrading and brushing away the rock from the fossil, so that the fossil stands in relief, proud of the surrounding rock. Like all such work, it demands great patience. Regular pauses help, to consider and discuss the work with others.*

BRUSHING AND CHIPPING

Sometimes all that is needed is a brisk dusting with a stiff brush, or a wash in water and detergent, using a soft scrubbing brush. A wire brush is tougher, but marks soft fossils.

Fossils embedded in highly layered shales may be exposed by carefully splitting the slab along its bedding plane.

If you need to remove rock matrix, test your technique on an area away from the specimen. Chip gently with a small bradawl or rock chisel and a small hammer. Or scrape carefully with a small pick, mounted needle, dentist's probe, or fine screwdriver. The fossil must be held firmly. Aim the force of your blows mainly downwards.

Power tools include small drills or burrs, as used by modelmakers, engravers and dentists. Beware of flying chips and shards they produce.

Do not rush. One false move could damage a valuable find.

OTHER METHODS

Some small fossils are lighter than their dense, heavy matrix. Try separating them by flotation on water or mineral oil. This could be combined with separation by swirling them in a sieve or bowl, as though panning for gold. Some fossils can be separated by using a vibrating tool or by alternate heating and cooling. Chemicals can also be used, but substances such as acids are powerful and corrosive. It is vital to get expert help for these specialist techniques, to take all safety precautions, and to follow the manufacturer's instructions.

Displaying Your Collection

A FOSSIL COLLECTION SHOULD BE dynamic and developing, as it changes with fresh finds, new identities for old specimens, and the latest theories about dating and evolution.

Cleaned fossils rarely need any further treatment for display. If they are very fragile, they can be preserved with specialist adhesives or resins, available from geology suppliers. Follow the instructions carefully, under the supervision of an expert. Do not put the display in direct strong sunlight or a damp place.

THE DISPLAY

You can make your own containers for your fossils, buy new ones, or adapt old closets, trays, drawers, packing cases, or boxes. The only limitation is your own ingenuity and ability to adapt.

Each fossil can be cushioned with cotton balls, wadding, bubble-wrap, or similar padding for protection. A card or label carries its catalog number, main identification in common and scientific names, and perhaps other information. The labels can be printed

WOODEN DISPLAY CASE *(below) has a fine array of mainly molluscan fossils, including ammonoids, plus some trilobites and othe arthropods. Specimens can be positioned in their natural groupings, or simply arranged to please the eye.*

DISPLAYS AND DRAWINGS *(above, right) were produced in the nineteenth century, when fossil-hunting was a fashionable pastime of the rich and famous. Such material can be found at sales and auctions.*

from a computer file, or drafted in elegant handwriting.

The catalog number refers viewers to the main notebooks, drawings, photographs, and database, for detailed information. If possible, write or paint the catalog number directly on the fossil, in a less visible area, using indelible ink or paint.

DISPLAY THEMES

You can boost your display's interest by arranging specimens around themes, perhaps adding your own illustrations and photographs. These include:
• Systematics—according to taxonomic (classification) groups of plants and animals.
• Chronology—working through time, from one geologic period to the next.
• Geography—from the regions where the fossils were found.
• Ecology—which animals and plants would have lived together in a community, for example, on an ancient seashore.

A NAME THAT LIVES FOR EVER

If you find a truly new kind of fossil, donate it to a museum. They will publish descriptions of it in scientific journals, and probably keep it in their collection, as the original or "type" specimen of its kind. In return, they may give you a replica of it. Its new scientific name may be based on your own name—which will live for ever!

Identifying Fossils: Plants
The First Plants

BIOLOGISTS GROUP, OR CLASSIFY, all living things into five broad categories. These are called the Kingdoms and the same classification is used for fossils. Of the five Kingdoms, the Monerans and Protists are microscopic in size, while the fossils of the soft-bodied, short-lived Fungi Kingdom are incredibly rare. So for most fossil hunters, the two Kingdoms of Plants and Animals are the most important. However, it helps to know about other Kingdoms, to understand the development of life on Earth.

MONERANS

These microscopic, single-celled life-forms comprise mainly bacteria and cyanobacteria, sometimes called blue-green algae. Their distinguishing feature is that their cells lack a distinct control center, or nucleus. Such cells are known as prokaryotic. This feature shows up in microfossils inside extremely ancient rocks. It reveals that monerans were the earliest life-forms on Earth, thriving in the seas over 3,500 million years ago.

Cyanobacteria can trap the energy of sunlight by the process called photosynthesis. This produces oxygen. So the early cyanobacteria helped to change the Earth's atmosphere from a

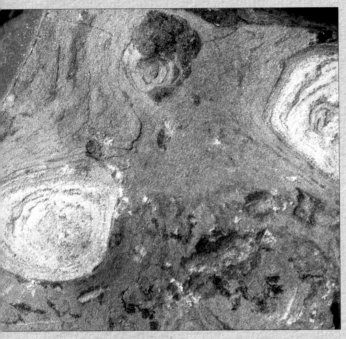

STROMATOLITES

(above) were made by millions of microscopic cyanobacteria (blue-green algae), in shallow sea water. Each layer produced limestone particles and trapped mud. Another layer grew on top, and so on, like huge stacked plates.

COLLENIA *(right) formed cone-shape stromatolite mounds up to 10 ft (3 m) high. Under the microscope, original algal cells can be seen fossilized as fine threads.* **Collenia** *lived in the tidal zone of tropical Precambrian seas.*

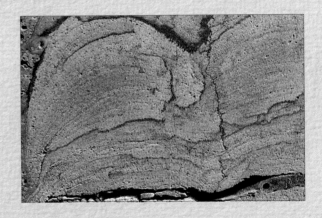

FIELD NOTES
• *Most of the early organisms on Earth were very small and so left only microfossils. Special equipment is needed to detect and identify them.*
• *Stromatolites consist of layers of rock such as limestone or silica, often in light and dark bands, in domes or mounds. Some are as big as dining tables.*

mixture of poisonous gases, such as methane and ammonia, to an atmosphere richer in oxygen, in which other living things could evolve. Bacteria and cyanobacteria still thrive today, in almost all environments on Earth, from the superheated water of hot springs, to inside icebergs.

PROTISTS

As oxygen built up in the Earth's prehistoric atmosphere, around 1,000 million years ago, new types of microscopic cells began to appear. Microfossils show that they were eukaryotic— each cell contained a control center or nucleus. The first types were protists, one-celled life-forms that still thrive in their billions today, mainly in the sea, fresh water, and moist soil. They can trap sunlight like plants, or take in nourishment like animals, or both! Many of them can move about actively, by wriggling or by waving hair-like filaments, and some have shells. Protists lived in such numbers that their fossilized shells and remains piled up deeply on the seabed, and eventually formed rocks such as chalk. Their shell shapes make them ideal indicator or guide fossils—if you have a microscope to study them.

COOKSONIA *(above) was an early dry-land plant (see p. 38). Its stiff stem contained tubes to carry water up to its 'branches'. Each tip sprouted a capsule containing hard-coated microscopic spores.* **Cooksonia** *grew in Silurian and Devonian swamps all over the world.*

THE APPEARANCE OF PLANTS

Plants are multi-celled living things that make their own food using the energy they trap from sunlight, in the process called photosynthesis. The first plants were algae or seaweeds. They were soft and floppy, so their fossils are very rare. They included green, red, and brown algae.

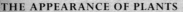

FOSSILS OF ALGAE *come in many forms. The two polished sections (sliced surfaces) of rock show layers formed by algal filaments of* **Collenia** *(above, top) and* **Girvanella** *(above, middle). The three lumps of coralline algae (above, middle and bottom) formed their own stony skeletons.*

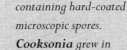

ALGAE *(left) lack true roots or a vascular system of internal water-transport pipes. So they must live in damp places. They range from microscopic hair-like filaments to seaweeds like giant kelp.*

Plants Invade the Land

Plants were the first living things to emerge from water onto land. The earliest plants were probably mats of green algae that lived around the edges of pools and lakes. But algae are soft and floppy, and soon dry out. In order to survive, they needed to evolve a more waterproof body covering, or cuticle, stiffened body parts to hold and support themselves, and tubes to take in water and nutrients and transport these around within their bodies. These last two features were combined as a network of pipes and tubes, called the vascular system, inside the plant.

PSILOPHYTES AND RHYNIOPHYTES

These were the first true land plants, such as *Cooksonia* and *Rhynia*, from the Silurian Period, about 420–400 million years ago. They were a few inches long and similar to the "whisk fern" *Psilotum* alive today. Some formed branching networks with vertical "stalks." Their fossils are rare.

LIVERWORTS AND MOSSES

Bryophyta

By 400 million years ago, some tiny matlike growths of algae had hairlike projections on the underside, called rhizoids, for soaking up rain water from the land. These were early types of roots.

Liverworts are known from Devonian times, over 360 million years ago. Like today's types, they had fleshy, rounded bodies with spore-bearing stalks.

ANNULARIA

(left), a horsetail, had whorls of ribbon-like leaves growing from regular sites, nodes, along its stem. Fossil leaf whorls are often found separated from stems. Some leaves bear spore cases and some stems have cone-like structures.

Mosses first appeared about 300 million years ago, in the swampy forests of the Mississippian and Pennsylvanian (Carboniferous) Periods. Fossils show their soft. rounded leaflets carried on stems, forming creeping mats, trailing curtains, or dense cushions.

CLUB MOSSES, HORSETAILS AND FERNS

Pteridophyta

Club mosses, Lycopsida, appeared in the Mississippian (early Carboniferous) Period. They soon evolved into huge plants resembling palm trees, some over 100 ft (30m) tall, with tough, woody stems topped by large mosslike leaflets. Horsetails, Sphenopsida, had a single tall stem with regular umbrella-like rings of narrow leaves. They were similar in size to the club mosses. Ferns, Filicopsida, lived on the forest floor in the shade of giant club mosses and horsetails. They sprouted delicate fan-shaped or leafy fronds from a central stem. Some evolved into tree ferns with thick, woody stems, about 65 ft (20m) tall. The stem differed from a true tree trunk in that it had no bark, could not increase in girth, and had a limited root system. The fronds grew from the top like an umbrella.

In the Pennsylvanian (late Carboniferous) Period, massive forests of club mosses, horsetails, and tree ferns flourished in the vast, steamy swamps. Their fossilized remains form the coal burned today.

CLUB MOSSES, HORSETAILS AND FERNS *(above) survive today—most are only small, compared to their prehistoric tree-like relatives.*

PECOPTERIS *(below), a tree fern, had huge fronds of leaflets split two or three times. It grew 14 ft high in warm, wet Pennsylvanian (late Carboniferous) and Permian forests.*

FOSSILS OF EARLY PLANTS *(above) include two impressions of the horsetail* **Equisetum** *from Jurassic rocks; a cone of the club moss* **Sigillariostrobus** *in Carboniferous coal; a frond of the Triassic fern* **Cladophlebis** *from Tasmanian coal measures; and a Carboniferous impression of a stem of giant horsetail,* **Calamites**.

Plants with Seeds

THE PLANTS ON THE previous pages reproduced and spread by means of spores. These form in a different way to true seeds, which most plants produce today by means of cones or flowers that bear pollen grains (male sex cells) and eggs (female sex cells).

The fossil record contains various types of cone-bearing or coniferous plants, many of which are now extinct. They are grouped as the *Gymnospermopsida* ("naked-seed") plants. In particular, the seed ferns and cycads, along with the tree ferns (*see p. 39*) formed great forests during the Pennsylvanian (late Carboniferous) Period, up to about 280 million years ago.

ALETHOPTERIS *(above), a seed-fern, grew 15 ft high in the late Carboniferous and early Permian swamps. Large leaf fronds sprouted from the branches topping its fibrous trunk. The veined leaflets were often joined at their bases.*

PROGYMNOSPERMS

The progymnosperms included groups such as the *Cordaitales* and *Bennettitales*. They had woody stems up to 100 feet (30m) tall, and branches with fernlike leaves. The Cordaitales evolved in the Mississippian (early Carboniferous) Period, had simple conelike structures for reproducing, and died out by the end of the Permian Period. The Bennettitales evolved during the Triassic Period, had reproductive structures that were softer and more leafy, almost like flowers, and became extinct by the Cretaceous Period. Neither group produced true seeds.

SEED–FERNS
Pteridospermales
These were the first true seed-producing plants. They appeared in Devonian times and became extinct by the Cretaceous Period, but their descendants, the cycads, still survive. They may have also been the ancestors of flowering plants (*see p. 44*).

PTERIDOSPERMALES *(above) or seed ferns were the first plants with seeds and pollen. They no longer needed damp conditions to reproduce and they thrived for millions of years.*

ALETHOPTERIS *(above) was a Carboniferous seed fern. Unlike real ferns, it reproduced by seeds and not spores.*

FIELD NOTES
• Ferns (see page 38) and seed-ferns are difficult to distinguish from fossils of their leaves alone.
• Accurate identification depends on detailed leaflet shape, vein pattern and attachment to the stem, or rachis.

They had fernlike, leafy fronds branching from a single, woody stem, and produced seeds in structures made from specialized leaves at the ends of particular branches. Some grew to 16 feet (5m) tall. The fossils of their different body parts are usually found separately, and they have been given different names, even though they are from the same plant. This makes their classification extremely complicated.

CYCADS
Cycadiodales

Appearing in the Pennsylvanian (late Carboniferous Period), cycads were once a hugely successful plant group. But they declined about 150 million years ago, and are now scarce and limited to the tropics. They were mostly squat plants resembling squashed palm trees, with a short, woody, scaly-looking stem (looking like a large pineapple) and large leaves; each with a central stem and two rows of straplike fronds. They produce seeds inside cones.

THE GONDWANA TREE (left), **Glossopteris**, had delicate, finely-veined leaves. It produced its pollen and seeds in capsules called fructifications, growing on specially adapted leaves.

GLOSSOPTERIS (below) was a tree-sized seed-fern whose fossils are widely scattered across the southern continents. They show that these landmasses were joined as the supercontinent Gondwanaland, hence its name: Gondwana tree.

CYCADIODALES (above) were palm-like plants which produced their seeds in cones. They flourished during the Mesozoic Era.

Coniferous Plants

GINGKOS AND MODERN conifers such as pines and firs were once the dominant plants on Earth. With their tough bark, seed-bearing cones and generally narrow, spiky, or scaly leaves, they have been fossilized and preserved as whole "petrified forests." They flourished during the Age of Dinosaurs, in the Jurassic and Cretaceous Periods, and fed many of the large plant-eating dinosaurs (*see pp. 72-73*).

THE SPRUCE

(above) from Oligocene rocks in Washington, U.S. produces long, pendulous cones, and is a tall conifer which tolerates a range of soil types and low light levels.

CONIFER TREES

(above) generally have tough, sharp, needle-shaped leaves but some have broad leaves.

GINKGOS
Ginkgoales

Like the modern maidenhair tree, early ginkgos had woody stems and branches, and distinctive fan-shaped leaves. They appeared in the Triassic Period and flourished all over the world during Jurassic times.

MODERN CONIFER TREES
Coniferales

The first members of this group appeared alongside the early reptiles, in the Permian Period. They evolved into many different forms, such as monkey puzzles, pines, firs, redwoods, spruces, larches, and yews. Their numbers declined as the flowering plants took over in the late Cretaceous Period. But many still thrive in mostly cooler climates today.

The typical conifer tree has a tall, woody trunk with side boughs that fall or break off as it grows, and a branching top part or crown. Douglas firs and redwoods are the tallest of all trees, growing to heights of 330 ft (100m) or more.

PETRIFIED FORESTS

(left) are trees turned to stone. Their wood has been replaced by rock minerals, which in some cases include beautifully coloured agates and opals.

FOSSILIZED PINE CONE (left) with real pine cones and other woody parts of trees are preserved more often than delicate leaves and flowers—they sometimes survive so well that they seem to have just fallen from the tree.

FIELD NOTES
• *Conifer wood, or softwood, can be distinguished from hardwood because it is more uniform in texture and appearance, and its growth rings are relatively wide.*
• *However, identifying the exact type of fossil conifer wood can be difficult. This usually requires a microscope, or associated fossils such as needle-leaves or cones.*

Different parts of conifer trees are preserved as fossils, and include:
• The softwood of the bark, trunk, and stem, with its pattern of dark and light circles called growth rings.
• The scaly or needlelike leaves, which do not show a branching pattern of thickened veins as found in the angiosperms (*see p. 44*).
• Small male cones, which may resemble catkins or buds, and produce pollen (male sex cells).
• Larger female cones, which begin as budlike swellings—they house the ovules or eggs (female sex cells) and, when fertilized by pollen, develop into larger woody cones, with scales that open to release the seeds.
• Seeds, which developed from the ovules. They often have winglike extensions to help them float in the wind to new areas.

Amber

MANY CONIFERS CONTAIN A fluid within their pipelike transport system, called resin (rosin).
If the bark is damaged, it oozes out, thick and sticky, to seal the tree's "wound" and deter insects, germs, and other pests. Lumps of this may become fossilized as a golden-yellow substance called amber. This can contain bits of leaves, twigs, bark, seeds, and animals such as insects that became trapped—all preserved in perfect detail.

AMBER (above) appeared in the fossil record from the Cretaceous Period, although other types of preserved resin occur in older rocks. The Baltic Region and Dominican Republic have rich resources.

Flowering Plants

THE VAST MAJORITY of plants today belong to the group called Angiosperms or "covered seeds"—commonly called the flowering plants. They include most of the familiar grasses, herbs, flowers, bushes, and trees other than conifers. The angiosperms first appeared during the Cretaceous Period, perhaps 130 million years ago, and rapidly came to dominate the land vegetation. They may have evolved from a gymnosperm or a seed fern. Their spread occurred at the same time as insects were evolving rapidly. Most angiosperms transfer their pollen by means of insects, such as bees, ants, butterflies, beetles, and flies.

BEECH *(above) has been common in northern deciduous forests since the end of the Cretaceous Period. Its leaves are quite tough and fossilize well. So do its seeds, the familiar beech nuts or beech mast.*

FLOWERS
The unique feature of an angiosperm is its reproductive part or flower. These soft, delicate structures form fossils only very rarely. They are known mainly from impressions in soft mud or from being preserved in amber.

OTHER ANGIOSPERM FOSSILS
More common are fossils of angiosperm parts such as bark and wood, the tough-coated seeds, the microscopic pollen grains, or the hard, stiff network of veins in the leaves. This evidence coupled with studies of flower

LAUREL LEAVES
(right) are tough and waxy, break down slowly, and so make good fossils. Laurels were common in the Oligocene and Miocene Epochs of the middle Tertiary. They are evergreen, shedding leaves randomly and continuously rather than during one season.

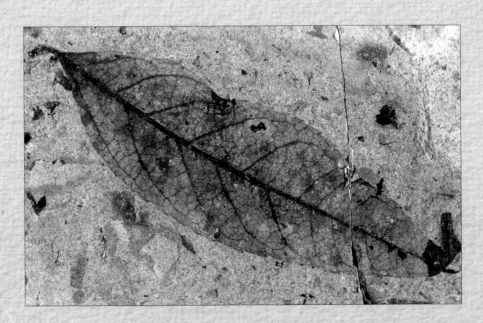

AN ELM LEAF *(right) beautifully preserved in Eocene rocks from Colorado, U.S. Like all deciduous trees, elms drop their leaves in winter—fossilization occurs only in unusual conditions, such as when fresh leaves are rapidly buried in stagnant mud.*

structure, suggests that the first angiosperms resembled magnolias (*Magnoliaceae*) and water lilies (*Nymphaceae*). Fossils of magnolialike flowers are found in rocks 100 million years old.

GROUPS OF ANGIOSPERMS

There are two main groups of angiosperms. The Dicotyledons have seeds which each contain two stores of food, called seed leaves or cotyledons. These provide nourishment to the baby plant during its early growth. Also, their leaves have branching networks of veins. They make up the great majority of angiosperm s.

The Monocotyledons have seeds which each contain only one seed leaf or cotyledon. They also have a network of parallel leaf veins. They include palm trees, lilies, and all types of grasses. The spread of the grasses came about relatively recently, during the Miocene Epoch, from about 25 million years ago—the same time that hoofed, grazing mammals (ungulates) also became very numerous.

POLLEN GRAINS *(above) are like micro-sculptures, each with a shape and surface decoration typical of its species. They can only be examined closely with the aid of a microscope.*

POLLEN MICROFOSSILS

One male flower can produce millions of microscopic pollen grains. Under the microscope, these have beautifully intricate shapes and surfaces. Pollen grains and spores are often preserved as microfossils, for example, in amber or sandstone. They are so common and characteristic that they can be used as indicator or guide fossils (*see p. 17*).

Identifying Fossils: Invertebrates
The First Invertebrates

THE FIRST TRUE animals probably appeared over 1,000 million years ago, evolving from microscopic, single-celled ancestors. Perhaps one-celled organisms in a loose colony began to change and adopt specialized roles, such as obtaining food, giving physical support, reproducing, and so on. Slowly individual colonies evolved into simple metazoans, or multicelled organisms. The first animals were almost certainly very small and jelly-like or soft-bodied. So their fossils are rare and hard to identify. However, they continued to change or evolve, giving rise to the many animal groups that have existed through time.

INVERTEBRATES AND VERTEBRATES

The animal kingdom is divided into groups called phyla. There are about 20 "major phyla" containing well-known animals such as insects and starfish. There are also another 20 "minor phyla" comprising fewer, lesser-known creatures, mainly wormlike animals of the deep sea. All but one of the major and minor phyla contain invertebrates—animals without true backbones. Invertebrates like mollusks and crustaceans

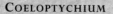

COELOPTYCHIUM *(right), a mushroom-shaped sponge, grew in Cretaceous northern seas. Even the spoke-like radial grooves on its underside resemble the gills of a mushroom.*

SPONGES *(above) still thrive in salty water, from shallow seas to the deepest ocean floor, and also in the fresh water of lakes and rivers.*

FIELD NOTES
• *Some sponges resemble plants, rather than animals. They had irregularly branching stems, like tree twigs.*
• *Other sponges may be confused with corals (see page 50) and the simple plants called calcareous algae, forming shapes resembling fans, antlers and mushrooms.*

SPONGE *(left) such as Cretaceous **Raphidonema** were filter-feeders. Corals (below left) such as Pliocene **Caryophyllia** caught food by sticky tentacles.*

evolved hard parts such as shells. These form excellent fossils. Some were so common that certain rocks, like shelly limestone, consist almost entirely of their fossils and remains.

SPONGES
Porifera

Among the simplest, and possibly earliest, animals were the sponges. Their fossils first appeared over 700 million years ago in the ancient seas. A sponge is basically a spherical or finger-shaped bag formed from a double layer of cells. It has no brain or nerves, and cannot move around. The bag's walls may have many folds with canals and chambers inside, and tiny holes or pores. Water passes through the pores into the main bag cavity, then out through a larger hole near the top. Cells lining the canals and pores cause the water to flow by waving their tiny hairlike projections. Nutrients floating in the water are taken in by cells lining the canals and cavities.

THE SPONGE SKELETON
Sponges formed fossils because their bodies were supported by a "skeleton" made of tiny, hard fibers, which were based on minerals containing calcium or silica, or tough proteins. When the sponge died, its skeleton was left as a hard object in the shape of the original animal, with a network of tiny holes and channels inside—the original "sponge." Some prehistoric sponge skeletons built up as rocky reefs, like coral reefs. The four main kinds are:
• Demospongea: with horny protein skeletons.
• Hyalospongea: glass sponges with silica-based skeletons.
• Calcispongea, with calcium or lime-based skeletons.
• Sclerospongea, the reef-building sponges.

SPONGES *(right) spread as mats, others grow as tall towers. They colonize new areas by releasing tiny swimming larvae into the sea.*

SIPHONIA *(above) was a pear-shaped "sponge-on-a-stick", attached by a basal root-like holdfast. Pores opened into the internal gastric cavity, where food was absorbed.*

Simple Creatures

THE PROTISTS ARE single-celled organisms in the kingdom Protista, one of the five main Kingdoms for all living things. Some grow like plants, using the energy in sunlight (*see p. 37*). Others are more like microscopic animals, taking in minute particles of nutrients. They were formerly called protozoans, and they survive in every damp or wet habitat in the world.

SINGLE-CELLED "ANIMALS"
Protists

Certain animal-like protists make beautifully sculptured shells, called tests, for protection. They float in the plankton of oceans and lakes, and when they die, their tests sink to form microfossils and deep layers of sedimentary rocks. These remains go back 700 million years. The main groups include:

• Foraminiferans and Nummulites, with calcium-based, chalky shells.
• Radiolarians, with silica-based, glassy shells.
• Ciliates, with lots of tiny hairlike cilia all over their bodies.

GRAPTOLITES
Graptolithina

Graptolites were tiny wormlike creatures that fed by means of a tentacled, funnel-shaped body part, the lophophore, that filtered minute nutrient particles from the sea water.

"TUNING FORKS"
(above) in the rocks are really fossils of the graptolite **Didymograptus**. *This lived in northern seas during Ordovician times, and the twin-armed colonies grew to the size of human fingers.*

RASTRITES
(left) was a monograptolite, meaning that the colony had one ("mono") curved stalk or stipe. Relatively few thecae — the shells of the individual organisms — branched off this stipe. **Rastrites** *fossils are often found in Silurian shales made from deep sea ooze.*

NUMMULITES (left) formed the rock used to build the Ancient Egyptian Pyramids. **Monograptus** (above) had many different forms and is an important indicator for Silurian times.

Graptolites thrived in their billions from the Cambrian to the Mississippian and Pennsylvanian (Carboniferous) Periods, then died out. Each individual made a cup-shaped shell for itself. The shells formed multibranched colonies (rhabdosomes), like bushy necklaces, that floated in the sea. After death, the strings of shells formed plentiful fossils.

GRAPTOLITES (above) were possibly distant relatives of marine worm-like creatures living in branched tubes today, called pterobranchs.

Graptolites were found in all the world's oceans, and their fossils form squiggles in the rocks that look like unsteady handwriting. The name grapto-lith means "written rock." The shell shapes and branching patterns changed through time and are very distinctive. They can be used as indicator or guide fossils for dating rocks (see p. 17), especially those of the Ordovician and Silurian Periods.

MOSS ANIMALS OR SEA MATS
Bryozoans

These tiny anemonelike animals live in colonies in sea water. Each makes a stony cup or box for itself out of rock minerals, much like a coral animal, and filters nutrient particles from the water. As the colony grows, it spreads in a characteristic pattern over a rocky surface or seaweed frond, looking like a hairy or mossy mat. Fossils of rows and groups of tiny, cuplike boxes are first found in Ordovician rocks. Bryozoans are still very common even today.

FENESTELLA (above), a bryozoan or sea-mat, formed a delicate conical network made of two rows of tiny calcareous boxes. Each box contained a coral-like animal or zooid.

Corals and their Relatives

The animal phylum called Cnidaria contains the corals, jellyfish, sea anemones, and hydras. These simple creatures consist mainly of a bag containing a stomach, with only one opening which works as a mouth and anus. This is surrounded by stinging tentacles that gather food.

JELLYFISH AND ANEMONES
Scyphozoa, Anthozoa
These animals appeared in the seas about 700 million years ago. Being mainly soft jelly, they were preserved only in exceptional circumstances, such as the impressions in soft mud. They are among the Ediacara fossils from late Precambrian times (*see pp. 8-9*).

CORALS
Anthozoa
Coral animals, called polyps, are like miniature sea anemones. Each polyp makes a limy shell, cup, or box for itself, and holds its tentacles out in the water, to sting tiny prey. Each generation of polyps builds on top of the shells of a past generation. The skeletons of thousands or millions of dead polyps build up into large structures that look like

---

ANCIENT ECOLOGY

Today's corals are very particular about where they grow. They need clear, shallow, unpolluted sea water, with a temperature of between 64°F (18°C) and 80°F (27°C). Presumably, in former times they were similarly fussy. So fossil corals indicate the sea's warmth, depth, and clarity at the time. This is one of the strands of evidence that builds up to give a picture of ocean ecology in prehistory.

FAVOSITES *(above) formed flattened coral mounds on shallow-water reefs, 400 million years ago. The calices, or individual polyp skeletons, are jammed closely together to give a honeycomb-like pattern.*

EDIACARA FOSSILS

Fossils found in the Ediacara Hills of southern Australia show an amazing snapshot of sea life around 700–600 million years ago. This was during late Precambrian times, and hard shells had not yet evolved. The soft-bodied animals such as jellyfish, seapens, anemones, and corals were probably smothered by a sudden chance covering of sand and preserved as fossils. Similar rare fossils are known from other sites, including northern Russia and Namibia in southwest Africa.

FIELD NOTES

• *Corals grow and spread in a wide variety of forms, making them awkward to identify.*
• *The surface of a piece of coral may show the cup-like skeletons or calices of the coral animals.*
• *Each calice may contain a set of star-like radial plates, like wheel spokes.*
• *Calices may be large and single, or tiny and joined with others in various patterns.*

CORALS *(below) grow in many forms—left to right,* **Halysites** *grew in chains;* **Heliophyllum** *was a solitary creature and formed a conical wrinkled or "rugose" calice;* **Favosites** *made a honeycomb effect;* **Heliolites** *grew in massive dense mounds.*

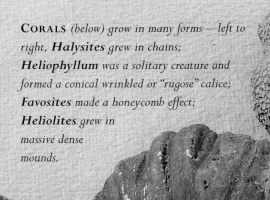

trees, bushes, fans, and even human brains! These, in turn, build up into the limestone juttings and overhangs of a coral reef. Coral reefs have been fossilizing in the seas for 700 million years. One of the first types was the soft coral or seapen *Charnia*. Others were shaped like upside-down pyramids (*Conularia*), antlers (*Millepora*), wrinkled bones (rugose corals), and chains (*Halysites*). Most are now extinct.

HALYSITES *(right) was a chain-coral from warm Ordovician and early Silurian seas. Its small polyps grew side by side and left a linked row of tubular calices or cup-skeletons, which resemble a chain when viewed from above.*

Brachiopods and Similar Shellfish

THE BRACHIOPODS OR "arm-feet" are also called lampshells, from the resemblance of their shells to the oil lamps used by the ancient Romans. At first sight a brachiopod resembles a bivalve mollusk such as a cockle or mussel. But it belongs to a quite separate group of creatures, the Phylum Brachiopoda.

A few species of lampshells survive today, but they were once far more common and widespread. The fossil record contains thousands of species, beginning in early Cambrian times, over 540 million years ago. These creatures evolved rapidly and the intricate details of their hard shells preserve well, making them useful as marker or guide fossils.

TWO-VALVED, NOT TWO-SHELLED

The two hard coverings of a brachiopod are not two shells, but two valves, or parts of a single shell. They do not cover the left and right sides of the creature, as in a bivalve mollusk, but the top and bottom.

The two valves of a brachiopod are not identical mirror images of each other, as they are in bivalve mollusks. A brachiopod's upper valve is smaller than the lower one, which often has an extended point or apex.

INARTICULATE BRACHIOPODS
Inarticulata

Fossils show that there were two main groups of brachiopods: the earliest was the Inarticulata, or "un-joined", and the other group was the Articulata or "joined". In the Inarticulata, the valves were not hinged, but held together only by muscles, so they could gape widely. After death, the muscles rotted and the valves fell apart, and so they fossilized singly.

TEREBRATULA *(above) was a fairly recent brachiopod, living about 10 million years ago in Europe. It has the two different valve shapes, with the point or apex of one curved around the other*

JOINTED VALVES *(above) of an articulate brachiopod have interlocking teeth and sockets, forming a hinge that links the two valves permanently. Inarticulate brachiopods lacked this structure, so the valves usually separated after death.*

LINGULA *(left), an inarticulate brachiopod, is named from its tongue-shaped valves. Some fossils show the concentric growth rings, like those of a tree-trunk, indicating the creature's age.*

FIELD NOTES

• *The two shell parts or valves of a brachiopod are usually different in shape, unlike those of a bivalve mollusc (see page 54).*

• *Also, each brachiopod valve is symmetrical, unlike a bivalve mollusc's valve, which may be lop-sided.*

• *One valve usually has a hole for the animal's stalk.*

FOSSIL BRACHIOPODS *(left) show the range of shell shapes these creatures developed. Left to right: the Jurassic plum-shaped* **Terebratula***; the conical* **Discinisca***, also from the Jurassic; the Devonian oyster-like* **Athyris***; the Jurassic scallop-shaped* **Rhynchonella***; the elongated* **Microspirifer** *from the Devonian Period.*

SPIRIFER *(above), an articulate brachiopod, lived from the Devonian to Permian Periods. Because of its worldwide distribution and characteristic valve patterns, it makes a good indicator fossil, especially in Mississippian and Pennsylvanian (Carboniferous) rocks.*

ARTICULATE BRACHIOPODS
Articulata

The other group, the Articulata, first appeared in the late Cambrian Period. The valves were held together by a hingelike structure, which persisted after death, so the valves were usually fossilized as a joined pair.

THE ANIMAL WITHIN

From the few remaining species of living brachiopods, we know that the animal inside the shell was quite different to a bivalve mollusk. Yet it lived a very similar lifestyle as a filter feeder, sifting tiny particles of food from the water. To do this, the brachiopod used paired, coiled feeding tentacles around its mouth, forming a structure called a lophophore or crown. Some types had a long stalk to anchor themselves in the mud. Others were attached directly to rocks or other hard objects by their shells.

TENTACULATES

Brachiopods belong to a varied group of invertebrate animals called Tentaculates. Other members that left fossils include bryozoans (*see p. 49*), and types of worms called phoronids that make hard protective tubes.

Mollusks 1: Bivalves

THE MOLLUSCS, COMMONLY called shellfish, are a huge phylum of varied animals including living types such as snails, slugs, whelks, limpets, mussels, cockles, tusk shells, cuttlefish, and octopus, and also several extinct groups known only from fossils, such as ammonoids. molluscs appeared in the seas during the early Cambrian Period, by 540 million years ago, and soon invaded fresh water too. Some 300 million years ago, in the shape of snails, they moved onto land.

Most molluscs have a soft body with a wrap-around fleshy "cloak," the mantle. This produces the tough, durable, protective shell, which increases in size as the animal grows. These shells form excellent fossils with finely preserved details, and mollusks are probably the most common animals in the entire fossil record. There are several main groups of mollusks . Four are described below and others are shown on the following pages.

MONOPLACOPHORANS
Monoplacophora
These small, crawling mollusks had low, limpetlike shells. They may have been the first mollusc an group to appear, and a few types still survive today in the deep sea.

CHITONS
Polyplacophora
Also called coat-of-mail shells, these small mollusks still live on seashores. They have a body and shell divided into many segments—a feature perhaps inherited from wormlike ancestor.

THIS OYSTER (above), **Liostrea**, *lived during the Jurassic Period in the UK. When settling as larvae, oysters may cement themselves onto older oysters.*

THE HINGE JOINT (above), *between a bivalve's two valves, is formed by teeth and sockets, linked in life by a strap-like ligament, which rots after death, letting the valves separate.*

DENTALIUM (below), *a tusk shell, has survived since Triassic times. It lives partly buried in the deep seabed of warm oceans.*

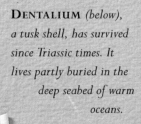

TRIGONIA (above) *lived partly buried in sand along Mesozoic coasts. This is a cast fossil, formed within the valves, which have since disappeared. The two large scars indicate positions of the valve-closing adductor muscles.*

MUSSELS *(left) such as* **Pinna** *still thrive today, in similar forms. This fossil came from the Cretaceous rocks of Sussex, U.K.*

FIELD NOTES

• *The two shell parts or valves of a bivalve mollusc are usually mirror-images of each other.*
• *However each valve is rarely symmetrical within itself, unlike a brachiopod valve.*
• *Most bivalves show muscle scars or attachments on the inside of each valve, one at each end.*
• *Oysters and their relatives have only one muscle scar in the centre.*

THE COCKLE

(right), **Ringicardium**, *looks almost exactly like the cockles of today's seashores. In some kinds, like* **Spondylus**, *the ribs extend as spines beyond the main shell edge.*

SCALLOPS *(below) included* **Flabellipecten** *and many similar forms (like* **Pecten**, *also shown below). These amazingly well-preserved specimens were found in Miocene rocks in France.*

TUSK SHELLS

Scaphopoda

These mollusks, with shells like elephant tusks, first appeared in Ordovician times. A few types still burrow in the mud on the deep seabed, where they feed on tiny creatures that they catch with their fine tentacles. The shell is tubular and tapering, and open at both ends.

BIVALVES

Lamellibranchia or Pelecypoda

These mollusks have a shell consisting of two hinged, mirror image parts, or valves. These can be clamped tightly together by muscles, or opened by relaxing the muscles, when an elastic ligament makes the valves gape.

Nearly all bivalves live in the sea, and they have thrived since Cambrian times. Many are familiar today on seashore rocks. Their valves make up a large proportion of the fossil record.

Bivalves are filter feeders, sifting particles of nutrients from the water. They have two tubes—siphons—for sucking in and expelling water. Some, like mussels, grow attached to rocks, others, like cockles, burrow in sand.

REEF-BUILDING MOLLUSCS

A group of bivalves called rudists lived about 100 million years ago in the sea. The lower valve was shaped like a cup or point-down cone, while the upper one functioned as a flattened lid. Rudists thrived in huge numbers and, like corals, they built great rocky reefs. They became extinct by the end of the Cretaceous Period.

Mollusks 2: Gastropods

GASTROPOD MEANS "stomach-foot," and gastropod mollusks seem to slide along on their bellies. The main types of gastropods are the thousands of kinds of snails with their twisted-spiral shells, and slugs, which have a smaller shell inside the body—or no shell at all.

Fossilized shells show that gastropods have flourished since Cambrian times, and invaded the land during the Pennsylvanian (Late Carboniferous) Period. Evolution has produced all sorts of shell shapes with intricate surface details and decorations (*see panel*).

ADAPTABLE SNAILS

Snails can withdraw into their shells, seal the opening with a "door flap" (the operculum) or with slime (mucus), and endure severe drought. Some are browsing herbivores, others are scavengers, while others still, like cone shells, are predators with a lethal poison "sting."

TWISTED BODY

To fit into a spiral shell, the basic mollusk body plan has been twisted around through 180°. This happens during the snail's early development and is known as torsion. It brings the mantle cavity (*see p. 54*) from the rear to the front, so that the snail can retreat into it and its shell when in danger. It also moves the shell away from the head, mouth, eyes, and other sense organs, and places it behind the snail for carrying along.

HIPPOCHRENES *(above), a European sea snail, had an elegant "skirt" extending from the shell aperture or mouth.*

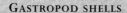

GASTROPOD SHELLS *(right) vary in form from the spire shell* **Turritella** *to the globular* **Natica** *and olive-like* **Oliva**—*shapes depend on the rate at which the opening increases in diameter.*

TURRITELLA *(right) has lived buried point-down in seabed mud since Cretaceous times. The shell is long, and spire-like, Unlike many gastropods, the final or body whorl, which the animal occupies, is not especially enlarged.*

FIELD NOTES

• *Gastropod shells are made of minerals such as calcium carbonate.*

• *They never have separate chambers within the shell, as do cephalopod shells (see page 58)*

• *The shell's thinner outer walls may be lost, leaving only the thickened central columnella, resembling a twisted drinking straw.*

PARTS OF THE GASTROPOD SHELL

As a young snail grows, it adds more material to the shell opening, to make the whorls bigger and wider. The shell usually twists in a clockwise direction when seen from the pointed end. The adult has a fixed number of whorls, the last and largest being the body whorl, where most of the snail's body is housed. Gastropod shells differ from the similar coiled shells of cephalopods (*see p. 58*) in that their interiors are not divided into chambers by internal walls.

Join between whorls—the suture

Pointed end—the apex

Smaller whorls

Mouth of shell—the aperture

PLEUROTOMARIA (*left*), *from the Jurassic rocks of Gloucestershire, U.K. is a typical snail-like gastropod combining spiral and helical (corkscrew-like) shell geometry.*

Shell covered with ridges, crests, ribs or spines

SNAIL SHELL SHAPES

The spiral shape of the gastropod shell has evolved into many further designs, all represented by fossils. These are:

• *Almost flat, like a coiled watchspring, as in the ram's-horn pond snail.*

• *Hemispherical or only one main half turn, like the seashore winkle.*

• *A very tall spiral, like a church spire, as in the spire shells of mudflats.*

• *Just one turn of the spiral, as in slipper shells.*

• *No spiral whorls at all, but an uncurled, straightened low cone, as in the seashore limpet.*

• *A loose spiral whose whorls do not join to each other, giving a spiraling tube effect, as in the extinct* **Orthonychia.**

LIVING GASTROPODS (*above*) *such as the snail carry their shells over their backs, crawling along by muscular waves which travel along the underside of the "foot".*

Mollusks 3: Cephalopods

CEPHALOPOD MEANS "head-foot." These mollusks all live in the sea. They have several tentacles around a beaklike mouth, and big eyes to spot prey and danger. They swim backwards by jet propulsion, squirting water out of a funnel-shaped siphon, and show complex behavior including the ability to learn.

Living cephalopods are the octopuses, cuttlefish, squid, and pearly nautilus. Extinct types, identified by their fossil shells, include other kinds of nautiloids, also belemnoids, and one of the best-known of all fossil groups, the ammonoids. Some Silurian nautiloids and ammonoids reached 13 ft (4m) long, and were the first really big animals.

NAUTILOIDS
Nautiloidea

Nautiloids are known from their fossil cone-shaped shells, marked by lines or ridges on the inside, called sutures. These were the joints between the delicate internal walls that separated the inside of the shell into chambers. As the creature grew, it occupied the largest, outermost chamber.

Nautiloids were the first cephalopods, appearing in late Cambrian times. They thrived mainly from the Ordovician to the Triassic Periods, about 200 million years ago. The early nautiloids were straight-shaped, but later ones had coiled shells. The vast majority are long extinct.

AMMONOIDS
Ammonoidea

These fairly large sea dwellers evolved from straight, cone-shelled nautiloids in the Devonian Period. They could retreat inside their shells like snails and close the opening with a doorlike lid, or aptychus. The coiled shell had complex sutures, patterned with saddles pointing forward (toward the opening) and backward-pointing lobes that show up well on many fossils.

There were several main kinds of ammonoids:
• Goniatites had jagged, angular, zig-zag sutures. They lived from the Devonian to the early Triassic Periods. They had disk-shaped shells, like flattened spirals. They are among the most frequently found and widespread of all fossils.

ACROCOELITES *(above), a common Jurassic belemnoid, left thick beds of fossil guards (the hardest part of the internal shell). Some of the guards are broken, revealing the chambered phragmocone within.*

SQUID *(above) are highly successful modern cephalopods, closely related to the extinct belemnites. The thin shell, or pen, is within the rear body. Giant squid are the largest of all invertebrates.*

FIELD NOTES
• *Cephalopod shells had inner chambers with dividing walls, unlike gastropod shells.*
• *Nautiloid shells were straight or coiled.*
• *Ammonoids were coiled early in their evolution, but later species had straight shells.*
• *Both had a "lid" to the main shell, a small conical structure called the aptychus, often found as a separate item.*

• Ceratites had wavy sutures, rounded saddles, and frilled lobes. They lived mostly during the Triassic Period. The shell has a narrow umbilicus (a central "pole" up the middle).

• Ammonites yielded some of the most common and familiar fossils from the Mesozoic Era. They vary from straight to spiral, and in size from 1–2 inches to almost 10 ft (3m) across. Appearing in the Triassic Period, they were very successful until the end of the Cretaceous Period, when they died out. Ammonite fossils are found in Mesozoic rocks, especially various limestones, all over the world. They are so common and evolved so rapidly that they are used as guide fossils.

BELEMNOIDS
Belemnoidea

These squidlike cephalopods had a three-part internal shell—of which the solid "bullet-shaped" part is usually preserved, its common name being "Belemnite bullet". Belemnoids evolved during the Mississippian (early Carboniferous) Period— most disappeared 65 million years ago. All are now extinct.

CENOCERAS (above), a nautiloid, swam in Triassic-Jurassic seas. This fossil has been sliced and polished to show the internal walls or septa between the chambers.

GASTRIOCERAS (below), a goniatite ammonoid, lived near the Mississippian (early Carboniferous) seabed and grew to about 4 in across. Tubercles (lumps) and ribs ornament the inner side of the shell whorls. But these do not reflect the internal structure of the chambers within.

CEPHALOPOD REMAINS (above and left) from left to right; the polished goniatite shows gently curving sutures inside its shell; a section of a typical ammonoid,

Bacculites, with one or two coils and a long, straight shell section; a typical ammonoid with its shell decorated with regular ridges; and a small goniatite fossil.

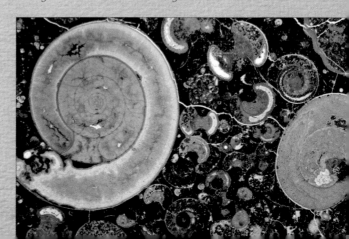

Arthropods 1: Trilobites and Crustaceans

ARTHROPOD MEANS "jointed leg." This vast group, the largest of all the animal phyla, includes creatures with a hard, outer body shell or casing, the exoskeleton. It is made of plates and tubes linked by hinges and joints, especially in the legs, for walking. Sea arthropods such as trilobites, crabs, and lobsters had thick exoskeletons that made good fossils. Land arthropods such as insects and spiders (*see pp. 62-63*) were smaller and had thinner exoskeletons, and were less likely to fossilize.

TWO-ENDED TRILOBITE (*above*) *Paralejurus* had head and tail shields of almost equal size. It lived in warm, shallow Devonian seas.

ARTHROPOD GROWTH AND MOLT ING

The plates and tubes of the arthropod exoskeleton are hard and rigid for protection and support. But they cannot enlarge as the creature grows. To overcome this problem, arthropods molt or cast off their body casings, leaving a new, softer one underneath that quickly enlarges and then hardens. So many fossils are not of the animals themselves, but of their molt ed casings.

TYPES OF ARTHROPODS

The first arthropods evolved over 600 million years ago, probably from soft-bodied, wormlike ancestors. It was once thought that all arthropods came from a single ancestral group, but many experts now believe that there were several groups, which evolved separately:
• Crustaceans, including the living barnacles, fish lice, water fleas, sandhoppers, sowbugs (woodlice), krill, crayfish, shrimps, prawns, crabs, and lobsters—all of which had prehistoric relatives.
• Uniramia, mainly the insects, centipedes, and millipedes.
• Chelicerata, chiefly spiders and scorpions, and king (horseshoe) crabs.
• Trilobites.

AEGER (*above*), a shrimp in Jurassic seas, was near the beginning of decapod evolution — the crustacean group including crayfish, crabs, lobsters and prawns. The rear limbs bear feathery paddles for swimming.

HOW TRILOBITES LIVED

Most trilobites probably had a crab-like lifestyle, crawling and scavenging for bits of food on the seabed. Some could burrow, others could swim by waving their limbs. Their bodies were divided into regular sections or segments, flattened from top to bottom, and ranged from the size of a rice grain to a size larger than a dinner plate. Each segment had a pair of jointed limbs, and they also had large eyes for seeing food and danger.

TYPICAL TRILOBITES AND CRAB FOSSILS— *larger (rolled into a protective ball) and smaller specimens (far right and top middle) of* **Phacops**—*had three tapering sections to its body, and a large-eyed head shield covered with nodules; wide-headed* **Leonaspis** *(bottom middle), another trilobite with body segments extended backwards as spines; and crab fossils (right) often found perfectly preserved inside rounded clay nodules.*

THE LOBSTER *(above), one of the largest living crustaceans, with a hardened exoskeleton. The only terrestrial crustaceans are woodlice (sowbugs).*

AGNOSTUS *(below), a Cambrian trilobite, smaller than a fingernail. It only had two thorax segments between its head and tail part, no eyes, and may have been a parasite.*

TRILOBITES
Trilobitomorpha

Trilobites were abundant in the seas from Cambrian times, and are among the most numerous animals that formed fossils. But they all died out by the end of the Permian Period, some 250 million years ago.

Trilobite means "three-lobed." Seen from above, the body casing or exoskeleton had two lengthwise furrows which formed three lengthwise ridges or lobes. From front to back there were also three body sections—a head shield or cephalon, a segmented main body or thorax, and a tail section or pygidium.

TRILOBITE VARIETY

More than 10,000 species of trilobites are known from fossils. As trilobites evolved, different types developed a huge variety of shell shapes and ridges, spines, distinctive eyes and tails, segment numbers and other features. So these crustaceans make good guide or marker fossils throughout the Palaeozoic Era, and especially the Ordovician, Silurian, and Devonian Periods.

Arthropods 2: Insects and Spiders

T HE FIRST ANIMALS to walk on land were arthropods. They were probably types of millipedes and lived about 400 million years ago. They evolved a waterproof exoskeleton to withstand exposure to air, fed on the decaying bits of land plants, and were safe from predators in water. However, almost as soon as they took to land, their predators (scorpions and centipedes) evolved to follow them.

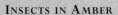

INSECTS IN AMBER

(above), or fossilized tree resin, preserves the minute details of its head, eyes, legs and even antennae. Material has been extracted from such fossils and analyzed for fragments of genetic or DNA content. But "recreating" a living organism is still science-fiction.

MILLIPEDES AND CENTIPEDES

Myriapoda

These earliest of land arthropods probably evolved from wormlike ancestors. Millipedes have two pairs of legs on each body segment and have existed since Devonian times, feeding on decaying plants. Some Mississippian and Pennsylvanian (Carboniferous) types grew to almost 6 ft 6 in (2m) long. Centipedes appeared soon after millipedes, as sharp-fanged hunters with one pair of legs on each body segment. Like millipedes, their exoskeleton sections sometimes form ringlike, C-shaped fossils.

INSECTS

Insecta

The first insects were tiny wingless creatures similar to today's springtails, one of the earliest being *Rhyniella* from the Devonian Period. The insects evolved rapidly, and by the end of the Pennsylvanian (late Carboniferous) Period most types had appeared. The largest winged insect ever, the dragonfly *Meganeura* of Pennsylvanian (late Carboniferous) swamps, had a wingspan of 27 in (70cm). There are two major groups of insects:

• The first were exopterygotes including dragonflies, cockroaches and termites. Their young are similar in body form to the adult.

• Endopterygotes

UNCOMMON FOSSILS

Fossils of small land arthropods like insects and spiders are generally rare. Their body casings or exoskeletons are mostly thin and fragile, easily broken by predators, scavengers, or weather. Also, they are uncommon because being covered quickly by fine mud or similar sediments, for detailed preservation, is far less likely on land than in water.

Small land arthropods were usually fossilized by chance burying under mud slides after a storm, or after falling into airless mud in stagnant water, where predation or decay was unlikely, or becoming trapped in amber (*see p. 43*).

FIELD NOTES

• *Because their body casings are fragile, fossils of arthropods like insects and spiders are rare.*
• *The few fossils form by burial under mud slides after a storm, or after falling into airless mud in stagnant water, where predation or decay was unlikely,*
• *Some are trapped in amber.*

appeared in the Pennsylvanian (Late Carboniferous) Period. They include beetles, flies, bees and butterflies. Their larvae change shape dramatically as they develop, a process called metamorphosis.

Insect fossils are generally rare (see panel). Most come from the last 60 million years, especially as bees, butterflies and flies evolved alongside flowering plants. The best specimens are in coal deposits or amber.

SPIDERS, SCORPIONS, AND KING CRABS
Chelicerata

Chelicerates are arthropods that first appeared about 560 million years ago in the seas. There name derives from their fang-like claws (chelae) in front of the mouth. Most have four pairs of walking legs. There have been several main groups through the ages, and all formed fossils.

• Eurypterids or water-scorpions appeared some 500 million years ago. Some grew to almost 10 feet long with fangs. They were the biggest hunters until the fish evolved.
• King or horseshoe crabs are not true crabs, but relatives of the eurypterids. They date back to Ordovician times and have a shield-like carapace and a spike tail. A few types still live today in coastal seas.
• True scorpions (one group of arachnids) evolved in the sea about 440 million years ago. They soon came onto land, as some of the earliest land predators.
• The first spiders (the other group of arachnids) developed about 370 million years ago. They fed on insects, but by chasing rather than spinning webs.

EURYPTERUS (*above*) *was a sea scorpion that terrorized mid-Paleozoic seas. The beetle below,* **Cybister***, was preserved when it landed in the famous La Brea Tar Pits of Los Angeles, California, where mammoths and saber-tooth cats were also entombed.*

LIBELLULA DRAGONFLY *(below) developed as dragonflies today—its fossils include the freshwater-dwelling larva. The libellulid dragonfly group includes skimmer and darter dragonflies still thriving today.*

HORSESHOE CRABS *(above) are not true crabs but relations of spiders. They are one of the main candidates for the name "living fossil," unchanged for over 200 million years.*

Echinoderms

ECHINODERMS ("SPINY-SKINS") are a very distinctive phylum of animals. They all live in the oceans and include starfish, brittlestars, urchins, sea lilies, and sea cucumbers. They are radially symmetrical in body plan, usually with spokelike arms or body sections, based on the number five.

The typical echinoderm has a protective and supporting skeleton of various-sized, six-sided chalky plates or ossicles, just under the skin. These fossilize well, but they tend to fall away separately as the creature decomposes. Many fossils are therefore of detached individual ossicles. Some echinoderms also have spines or lumps in their skin, which also fossilize well. The main living groups of echinoderms are all well represented in the fossil record.

STARFISH *(above) and their relatives first appeared in Ordovician rocks 500 million years ago and are one of the most successful marine invertebrates. This feather star,* **Saccocoma**, *is from Jurassic rocks, Germany.*

SEA LILIES AND FEATHER STARS
Crinoidea
Sea lilies, with a "crown" of food-gathering arms on a stalk, and feather stars, which are unstalked versions, live anchored on the seabed. They were among the first echinoderms from the Cambrian Period, and flourished in Carboniferous times. Sections of sea lily stalks are often fossilized as rows of disks or short rods.

STARFISH AND BRITTLESTARS
Asteroidea, Ophiuroidea
Starfish live in shallow water, moving by means of many tiny, waving tube feet on the underside. Brittlestars move by rowing with their long arms and live in dense mats on the deep seabed. Both groups date back to Ordovician times. Their ossicles are small, and become separate after death, so they are difficult to identify.

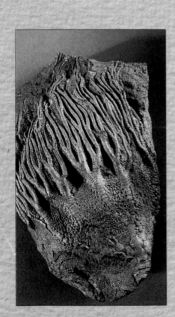

SCYPHOCRINITES *(left) was a crinoid, or sea lily, from 400 million years ago. The bulbous base of the stem may have functioned like a holdfast, anchoring it to the seabed. Or it may have been a float to suspend the animal in ocean currents. Five arms branched repeatedly to form a large calyx or crown.*

BRITTLESTARS *(above) gather food particles and pass these along their arm's food groove, towards the central mouth on the underside.*

FIELD NOTES

• *Most echinoderms show a symmetry (such as numbers of arms) based on five or multiples of five, which is otherwise rare in the living world.*

• *The external skeleton is made of calcite spines or plates, ossicles, that fall away as the flesh rots after death.*

• *Ossicles were so common that they formed the rock itself.*

SEA CUCUMBERS

Holothuroidea

These sausage-shaped echinoderms live on the deep seabed, filtering food from the mud. They have no spines and their ossicles are like tiny spikes, so their fossil remains are difficult to identify without a microscope.

SEA URCHINS,

or echinoids, are ball-shaped creatures with an outer shell. **Hemicidaris** (top) has large sculptured lumps or tubercles. In life, each was topped by a grooved spine. Sea urchins that move over the seabed, such as this modern specimen (bottom right), are usually spherical. Burrowing types such as **Micraster** (left) are two-sided, or bilaterally symmetrical.

SEA URCHINS

Echinoidea

Urchins are like starfish whose arms are bent upwards and joined along their sides and top to form a ball. The ossicles are fused together into a spherical shell known as a test, which has an intricate pattern of holes and lumps. Fragments of test often form fossils, as do the urchin's protective spines. An urchin has specialized scraping and chewing mouthparts formed from five strong, hard "teeth" moved by a lever system. This is known as Aristotle's lantern and it is very resistant, so it often fossilizes as a separate item. Most sea urchin remains are found in rocks from the Cretaceous and Tertiary Periods, from about 140 million years ago.

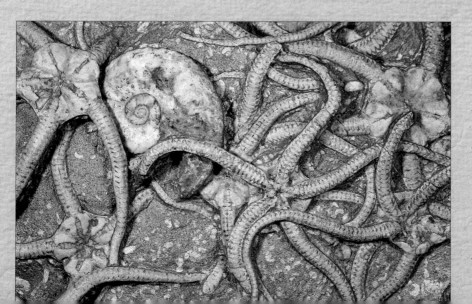

PALAEOCOMA (left), a brittle star, was common during the latter half of the Mesozoic Era. Its fossilized diamond-shaped central disc, minus the fragile arms, is found by the thousand. Modern brittle stars are extremely similar, crowding the seabed in thick carpets, catching edible particles from the water by waving their arms.

Identifying Fossils: Vertebrates
The First Vertebrates

THE APPEARANCE OF a backbone, or vertebral column, was a giant step forward in animal evolution. It gave a framework for the muscles on either side of the body to pull on, and flex it from side to side. Such a movement is ideal for swimming. This step also marked the appearance of true bone, forming skulls and skeletons, which are so important in the fossil record. The first vertebrates were fishes appearing worldwide in oceans some 500 million years ago.

JAWLESS FISHES
Agnatha
The early jawless fishes were often heavily armored, with large plates of bone embedded in the skin, giving the group name Ostracoderms ("shell-skins"). Most lacked the paired fins of modern fishes, though some had ridges and keels along the bony plates, and a finned tail. Ostracoderms lived worldwide, but died out some 350 million years ago. Most were only a few inches long, so their fossils are small and awkward to identify.

EARLY JAWED FISHES
Acanthodians
After the backbone, another great step forward was the evolution of hinged jaws. Fishes could now bite, chew, and become predators. The first jawed fishes were Acanthodians, also called spiny fishes. They appeared 400 million years ago and died out around 230 million years ago. They had several pairs of fins, with a sharp spine supporting each fin's front edge. The body was covered with stud-like scales. These fishes were only a few inches long, and they lived in fresh water; their fossils are rare.

CEPHALASPIS *(below) was smaller than a human hand. It lacked jaws and belonged to the ostracoderm group. Two holes in the head shield may have been for eyes.*

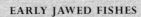

SKATES *(above) and rays are flattened members of the cartilaginous fish group, related to sharks— mostly specialised bottom feeders, they can swim gracefully by "flapping" their wing-like fins.*

TEETH
(left) and jaws did not occur in the first fishes, who had sucker- or rasp-like mouths and licked or scraped their food. Teeth appeared later, on jaws which evolved from one of the pairs of gill arches on the side of a fish's head.

SHARK'S TOOTH

The typical shark's tooth is thin and triangular, with a flatish base, slightly scooped with possibly serrated or saw-like sides, and a sharp-pointed top. Small ones, up to the size of fingernails, are very common. The biggest would almost cover a dinner plate.

EVEN AS FOSSILS *(above), sharks' teeth are fearsomely carnivorous. The larger is from* **Carcharodon***, a giant relative of today's great white shark. The smaller tooth belonged to an Eocene type of mako shark.*

ARMORED FISHES
Placoderms

Named for the body armor embedded in the skin at the front end, the Placoderms or "plated-skins" had wide-opening jaws edged with sharp blade-like ridges of bone, rather than true teeth. They swam mainly by wriggling, like eels. These fishes lived about 400–345 million years ago, and some grew to gigantic size. *Dunkleosteus* reached 33 ft (10m) in length!

CARTILAGINOUS FISHES—SHARKS AND RAYS
Chondrichthyes

Sharks, skates, rays, and chimaeras or ratfishes probably evolved from Placoderms around 390 million years ago. They were the dominant fish groups for hundreds of millions of years, and many survive today. Their skeletons are made of cartilage or gristle, which rarely fossilizes well, so few shark skeletons are preserved whole. Much more common are their fossilized teeth, which were coated with very hard enamel, or their scales (placoid scales), which were tiny versions of the teeth.

ODONTASPIS TEETH *(below) have tiny side cusps near the root. Close relatives of this Cretaceous shark prowled the seas in Devonian times, while other relatives do so today.*

Bony Fish

THE VAST MAJORITY of vertebrates alive today, over 20,000 species, belong to the group called Osteichthyes, the bony fish. Their skeletons have formed plentiful fossils, but the individual bones are often crushed or separated. A fossil fish skeleton found with the bones neatly laid out, and articulated or joined as in life (*see panel*), is a great prize.

There are two main groups of bony fish, the lobe-fins and ray-fins.

LOBE-FINS
Sarcopterygii

These fishes, also called tassel-fins, are named from the fleshy, stalk-like base of each main fin. The fin itself extends from this lobe and is supported by thin rods called fin rays. The fleshy lobes have bones inside, which can be seen in well-preserved fossils. The lobes can be moved like stumpy limbs, and it's probable that one of the main groups of lobe-fins, or tassel-fins, evolved into the four-legged amphibians. The grouping of lobe-fins is often hotly debated, especially with its significance for the vertebrate invasion of the land.

• Coelacanths were mostly large, deep-bodied lobe-finned fishes with a three-part tail. They were common from Devonian to Cretaceous times in fresh water, then in the oceans. Then they seemed to disappear from the fossil record…until a specimen was discovered in 1938 near the Comoros Islands in the Indian Ocean. Several coelacanths have since been studied

A COMPLETE FISH SKELETON (above) showing skull, jaws, backbone, ribs, and supporting fin rays is rare. This specimen has a single dorsal (back) fin on the right, with the pectoral and pelvic fins to the left.

LEPIDOTUS (right) could form its jaws and mouth into a tube, to suck lumps of food. This Jurassic holostean fish grew to more than 3 feet long. Usually only the chunky rhomboidal scales fossilized.

"FLAT"-FISH FOSSILS
*(left) are sometimes preserved
flattened between layers of
sediment. In life, the fish
would have been a normal
shape.*

FIELD NOTES

• *Bony fish skeletons may seem
tough as they scratch our
mouths and throats when we eat
fish. But they are mostly small
and fragile, and fossilize rarely.*
• *The bony spike-like rays in the
fins also fossilize, although they
may be confused with fish ribs.*
• *Fish otoliths also fossilize.
These are bony pebble-like
objects within the fish's balance
organs.*

and filmed in the region.

• Rhipidistians were a loose grouping
of long-bodied predators in Devonian shallow
freshwater pools. They could breathe air with lung-like body
parts, and were probable ancestors of the amphibians.
• Dipnoi, lungfishes could also—and can—breathe air and
survive drought. Their lobe-fins are small and weak. They
began in Devonian times, flourished during the Triassic, but
gradually faded. Only three types survive.

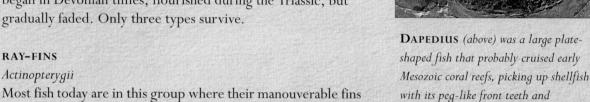

DAPEDIUS *(above) was a large plate-
shaped fish that probably cruised early
Mesozoic coral reefs, picking up shellfish
with its peg-like front teeth and
crushing them with grinding back teeth.*

RAY-FINS
Actinopterygii

Most fish today are in this group where their manouverable fins
are supported by bony rodlike rays which emerge directly from
the body, without the fleshy base of the
lobe-fin.

STURGEONS *(above) are
one of the few survivors of
an early bony fish group,*
Chondrostei. *Recently,
they have become even
rarer, killed for their
famous delicacy—caviar.*

The ray-fins first appeared about 370 million years ago, and soon
became more common than the Placoderms. Their fossils show they evolved
through the following series:
• Chondrosteans. These ray-fins had an upper tail lobe longer than the lower
one, long jaws, very thick scales, and bony plates as body armor. They
evolved in the Devonian Period and survive today as sturgeons and
paddlefish.
• Holosteans. They had a shorter upper tail lobe, thinner body scales, less
bony plates for armor, and shorter, more flexible jaws. They evolved in the
Triassic Period and are represented today by garpikes and bowfins.
• Teleosts. These are the great majority of modern bony fish. They have a
tail with equal upper and lower lobes, thin and flexible scales, and short
jaws which can be protruded or pushed forward to manipulate small food
items. They developed in the Jurassic Period.

Amphibians and Reptiles

AMPHIBIANS LIVE PARTLY IN water and partly on land. They evolved from fishes, and today include frogs, toads, salamanders, and newts. Most need water in which to lay their jelly-covered eggs, or spawn, which hatch into swimming larvae, tadpoles, which breathe using gills. They gradually developed four legs and moved out of the water onto land, and breathe with lungs.

Reptiles evolved from amphibians, and they had major new evolutionary developments such as a waterproof, scaly skin, a tough-shelled egg, and a more efficient limb design for easier walking and running. This meant they could break free of the water, and live entirely on dry land. Their bony skulls and skeletons yield better fossils than amphibians.

CACOPS (above), of the Permian Period in North America, thrived in the arid climate. Its body was covered with bony armour plates and it had strong legs, more like a reptile than an amphibian.

EARLY AMPHIBIANS

Amphibia

The first amphibian fossils date from late Devonian times, about 370 million years ago. The bones that supported the fleshy-based pectoral and pelvic pairs of fins in certain fishes (*see p. 68*), had become strong leg bones for the four limbs. These first amphibians had more curved, encircling ribs, to hold their internal organs away from the ground as they walked.

THE AGE OF AMPHIBIANS

Amphibians were the dominant land animals during Mississippian and Pennsylvanian (Carboniferous) times. They grew quite large, some over 10 ft (3m) long, and fed on insects and fish. Some evolved scaly or leathery, almost waterproof skin. The first frogs appeared 240 million years ago and were completely unlike earlier amphibians, possibly evolving separately from the main amphibian lineages. Since the later amphibians were small-bodied, with light, delicate skeletons, their fossils are rare.

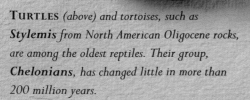

TURTLES (above) and tortoises, such as **Stylemis** from North American Oligocene rocks, are among the oldest reptiles. Their group, **Chelonians**, has changed little in more than 200 million years.

FROGS (left) and toads, newts and salamanders, and blindworms or cecilians, are the living representatives of the once-huge and widespread amphibian group.

TRIONYX *(left) was a mud turtle of Cretaceous lakes and slow rivers. Its descendants, soft-shelled turtles, still lurk in the same places. The bony shell plates were covered with skin, rather than horn as in other turtles.*

EARLY REPTILES
Reptilia

Reptiles first appeared about 300 million years ago, and dominated the land and seas throughout the Mesozoic Era. The first main group were the Cotylosaurs (stem reptiles). The hard-shelled eggs were likely to fossilize, giving a new type of object in the fossil record.

MAIN GROUPS OF FOSSIL REPTILES

Today there are three chief reptile groups. These are turtles and tortoises, or chelonians; lizards and snakes, or squamates; and crocodiles and alligators, or crocodilians. All have a long fossil history which, except for snakes, goes back to the Mesozoic Era. There were many extinct reptile groups that fossilized such as:
• In the sea, plesiosaurs, nothosaurs, ichthyosaurs, and mosasaurs (sea-going members of the lizard group).
• In the air, pterosaurs such as pterodactyls, plus some gliding lizards.
• On land, rhynchocephalians; including the pig-sized, beak-mouthed rhyncosaurs of the Triassic Period—one species of this group survives today, the lizard-like tuatara of New Zealand.
• Dinosaurs (*see pp. 72-73*).
• Mammal-like reptiles. Fossils suggest some may have had warm blood, body hair, and several types of teeth, like the descendants, true mammals.

VERTEBRAE *(below) are often found on their own, the rest of the skeleton having disappeared. This belonged to an ichthyosaur from Jurassic rocks in Yorkshire, England.*

ICHTHYOSAURUS *(left) swam in shallow northern seas during the Jurassic-Cretaceous Periods. Some fossils are beautifully preserved, showing the outline of its fins, tail and other fleshy parts.*

Ruling Reptiles: Dinosaurs

PROBABLY THE MOST FAMOUS of all prehistoric animals are the dinosaurs. The name means "terrible lizards," although they were not true lizards. They formed their own group of reptiles, the Dinosauria. They first appeared about 225 million years ago in the Triassic Period, reached their heyday in the Jurassic, ruled the land for 150 million years, then suddenly and mysteriously died out at the end of the Cretaceous Period, 65 million years ago.

Dinosaur fossils are quite rare, except in certain areas such as the Badlands of the American midwest and the Gobi Desert in Asia. They lived in dry areas, where fossilization was likely to occur, and their tough skeletons and bony horns and crests made noticeable fossils.

IGUANODON (above) was the second dinosaur to be identified from fossils. Its bones and teeth were found in southern England in the early 1800s. Large and heavy, it lived in herds and fed on tropical Cretaceous vegetation.

THE RANGE OF DINOSAURS

There were more than 350 basic types of dinosaurs ranging from delicate two-legged, two-armed upright runners, the size of robins, to giant four-legged lumberers weighing twice as much as a very big truck. There were two main groups, differing in the structure of their hips.

LIZARD-HIPPED DINOSAURS

Saurischia

The narrow hip bone called the pubis pointed to the front, with another bone, the ischium, to the rear. There were, in turn, various subgroups:
• Theropods ("beast-feet"). These included the earliest dinosaurs, the coelurosaurs, and *Deinonychus* and *Ornithomimus*. They were agile hunters. The carnosaurs were even bigger two-legged theropods, such as the fearsome *Tyrannosaurus* and *Allosaurus*.

NORTH AMERICA'S BADLANDS (above) are particularly rich in dinosaur fossils. During the Mesozoic Era, its climate and vegetation supported a great variety of dinosaurs and other animals. Today the area is dry and weather-beaten, ideal conditions to erode rocks and reveal fossils.

DINOSAUR TEETH (right and below) suggest diets. **Titanosaurus**, a huge plant-eater, had peg-like teeth for raking in vegetation (right). **Spinosaurus** had sharp fang-like teeth typical of a meat-eater (below).

Vertebrae (*right*) *of the larger dinosaurs had to be massive, to support the body's colossal weight. This is from **Iguanodon**, which probably walked mainly on its two back legs.*

• Sauropods were giant four-legged herbivores, with massive barrel-like bodies, long necks and tails, and tiny heads. They include *Brachiosaurus* and *Diplodocus*. They weighed tens of tons and their fossil footprints reveal that they lived in herds.

BIRD-HIPPED DINOSAURS
Ornithischia

In this group, the hip bone had both forward- and backward-pointing parts. They were mostly four-legged plant-eaters, but very diverse.
• Ornithopods, such as *Iguanodon*, *Pachycephalosaurus*, and the "duck-bills" like *Maiasaura*, could stand and run on their hind legs. They had flat grinding teeth. Fossils of their communal nest sites, eggs, and hatchlings show that some types had complex social and parental behavior.
• Stegosaurs had bony plates along their backs, possibly for controlling body temperature. They lived mainly during the Jurassic Period.
• Ankylosaurs like *Euoplocephalus* appeared in the Cretaceous Period and had large plates and lumps of armor.
• Ceratopians such as *Triceratops* had beaklike mouths, spikes and horns protruding from the face, and frill-like shields of bone over the neck.

Triceratops (*left*), *one of the last of the dinosaurs, had a huge bony neck-frill and three facial horns, to protect these plant-eaters from the carnivorous dinosaurs such as **Tyrannosaurus**.*

Dinosaur eggs (*above*) *formed various kinds of fossils. Some are the intact shells, preserved even in groups or clutches within a nest. Others have shells broken when the baby dinosaur hatched or the egg was crushed.*

Birds and Mammals

THE TWO MOST NOTICEABLE groups of animals today are the warm-blooded, furry mammals, and warm-blooded, feathery birds. However, apart from relatively few but concentrated sites, neither of these groups are especially common as fossils. Why?

LESS LIKELY TO FOSSILIZE

Birds and mammals became numerous only relatively recently in geologic time, mainly in the past 60 million years. Exposed surface rocks of this age, from the Cenozoic Era, are uncommon around the world, so finding the fossils is difficult. Also the total numbers of birds and mammals through time, compared to groups such as mollusks in the sea, have been small. And mammals tend to frequent habitats such as woodlands, where conditions for preservation are unlikely. The bony skeletons of many small mammals, and especially birds, are fragile and break and crumble, rather than fossilize.

BIRDS
Aves

The first known bird was *Archaeopteryx*, a combination of small dinosaur and evolving bird, from about 150 million years ago. It had jaws with teeth and a long bony tail, like a reptile, but possessed the unique bird feature—feathers.

Bird features which may fossilize include the toothless beak, front limb bones shortened into wings for flying, and the tail-less, fused vertebrae of the spinal column. Most bird bones are hollow, to save weight, which makes them more fragile and unlikely to fossilize.

ARCHAEOPTERYX *(above) had many features of a small dinosaur. But it also had feathers, the unique bird feature, beautifully preserved in fine-grained limestone.*

FOSSIL MAMMAL TEETH *(below), cave bear molar (left), and two types of prehistoric horse teeth (right), and a horse foot bone or metacarpal (below).*

HORSES
(above) have evolved from small, dainty, nimble forest dwellers to large, strong fleet-footed plains animals over a period of millions of years.

MAMMOTH MOLAR

TEETH *(right) grew through the animal's life, moving in pairs from the back to the front of the jaw, as in today's elephants. The owner was 15 feet tall and had 17-feet incisor teeth - its tusks.*

MAMMALS

Mammalia

The first mammals, small shrewlike creatures with furry bodies and warm blood, such as *Megazostrodon*, appeared alongside the first dinosaurs in the Triassic Period. Many prehistoric mammals are known only from their jaws and teeth.

Mammals stayed small and rare through the Mesozoic Era. With dinosaurs gone, they evolved rapidly into varied groups, from bats to rats, cats and dogs, horses and rhinos, monkeys and apes, and in the sea, whales and seals.

OTHER MAMMAL GROUPS

• Marsupials are pouched animals whose young are born at a very early stage of development and live in a pocketlike marsupium. They appeared 100 million years ago and spread to all continents.
• Hoofed mammals, called ungulates, evolved rapidly when grasses appeared, from about 25 million years ago. They included camels, cattle, deer, and horses, and have left a varied fossil record.
• Rhinos and tapirs were once a common, widespread group. They included the largest ever land mammal, *Paraceratherium*, more than 16 ft (5m) tall.
• Over half of the mammal species today are rodents, such as rats, mice, squirrels, and beavers. They first appeared 60 million years ago.
• The primates, including today's lemurs, monkeys, and apes, have a fossil history stretching back 40 million years. It's thought that apelike ancestors evolved into early humans in Africa, over the past 5 million years.

ELEPHANTS *(above) such as* **Mammuthus** *were once a widespread and varied mammal group. Today only two species survive.*

GLOSSARY

ANGIOSPERMS: plants, commonly called flowering plants, whose seeds have a protective covering.

APTYCHUS: the curved lid of an ammonoid shell.

CEPHALON: a shield that covers the head end of an animal such as a trilobite.

COLUMELLA: the central post formed where the whorls of a gastropod's shell join.

CONTINENTAL DRIFT: the movement of the rocky plates that carry the continental landmasses at the surface of the Earth's crust.

ENAMEL: a very hard substance that covers the teeth of many animals.

EVOLUTION: the gradual changes that organisms undergo over many generations so they remain suited to their environment.

EXOSKELETON: the outer hard covering of an animal such as an arthropod.

GASTROLITHS: stones which are swallowed by some animals and used to help grind food in the stomach.

GUARD: the hardest part of the internal shell of a mollusk such as a belemnite.

GYMNOSPERMS: plants, commonly called conifers, whose seeds do not have a protective covering.

INVERTEBRATES: animals without backbones.

KINGDOMS: the five divisions into which living organisms are grouped; Monera, Protista, Fungi, Plants, and Animals. Each Kingdom is in turn divided into groups called phyla.

METAMORPHOSIS: the change in body form which animals (such as amphibians) and some types of insects undergo as they mature.

MICROFOSSILS: fossils of organisms that can only be seen under a microscope.

OPERCULUM: the lid used to close a shell aperture.

OSSICLES: chalky plates embedded in the skin of animals such as echinoids.

OTOLITHS: small, round stones within the balance organs of vertebrate animals.

PALEONTOLOGIST: a person who studies fossils.

PERIOD: a unit of geological time marked by particular types of rock. Several periods make up an era. A period may be divided into epochs.

PHOTOSYNTHESIS: the chemical reaction carried out by green plants whereby light energy is absorbed and used to make food.

PLACOID SCALES: tiny teeth-like plates that cover the skin of sharks and their relatives.

PYGIDIUM: the tail section of an animal.

RADIOACTIVITY: the spontaneous atomic decay of certain substances which give off subatomic particles or rays.

REEFS: rocky structures under the sea made up of the chalky cases of tiny organisms such as corals.

SEDIMENTS: particles of eroded rocks deposited in layers that may eventually form sedimentary rocks.

SEGMENTS: the divisions of the bodies of many invertebrate animals.

SUTURES: lines marking the joins in a mollusk shell.

TEST: the hard shell of animals such as sea urchins.

THORAX: the central body section of an animal such as an arthropod.

TRACE FOSSILS: fossilized evidence of an animal's existence other than its body, for example its burrow, tracks, or droppings.

UMBILICUS: the center of a coiled shell.

VALVES: the two halves of the shell of an animal such as a brachiopod or a bivalve.

VERTEBRATES: animals with backbones.

WARM BLOODED: animals that maintain a constant body temperature regardless of the temperature of their surroundings. The body temperature of cold blooded animals fluctuates with the temperature of their surroundings.

WHORL: one turn of the shell of a spiral shell.

INDEX